1 & 2 Thessalonians
1 & 2 Timothy
Titus

ABOUT THE AUTHORS

General editor:

Clinton E. Arnold (PhD, University of Aberdeen), professor and chairman, department of New Testament, Talbot School of Theology, Biola University, Los Angeles, California

1 & 2 Thessalonians:

Jeffrey A. D. Weima (PhD, University of Toronto), professor of New Testament, Calvin Theological Seminary, Grand Rapids, Michigan

1 & 2 Timothy; Titus:

S. M. Baugh (PhD, University of California, Irvine), associate professor of New Testament, Westminster Theological Seminary in California, Escondido, California

Zondervan Illustrated Bible Backgrounds Commentary

1 & 2 Thessalonians 1 & 2 Timothy Titus

Jeffrey A. D. Weima
S. M. Baugh

Clinton E. Arnold   *general editor*

ZONDERVAN®

ZONDERVAN.com/
AUTHOR**TRACKER**
follow your favorite authors

Zondervan Illustrated Bible Backgrounds Commentary
    1 and 2 Thessalonians—Copyright © 2002 by Jeffrey A. D. Weima
    1 and 2 Timothy, Titus—Copyright © 2002 by Steven M. Baugh

Requests for information should be addressed to:

Zondervan, *Grand Rapids, Michigan 49530*

Library of Congress Cataloging-in-Publication Data
    Zondervan illustrated Bible backgrounds commentary / Clinton E. Arnold, general editor.
       p.cm.
    Includes bibliographical references.
    ISBN-10: 0-310-27823-6
    ISBN-13: 978-0-310-27823-8
    1. Bible. N.T.—Commentaries. I. Arnold, Clinton E.
    BS2341.52.Z66 2001
    225.7—dc21

       2001046801
       CIP

Printed in China

Interior design by Sherri L. Hoffman

07 08 09 10 11 12 13 • 12 11 10 9 8 7 6 5 4 3 2 1

CONTENTS

INTRODUCTION

All readers of the Bible have a tendency to view what it says it through their own culture and life circumstances. This can happen almost subconsiously as we read the pages of the text.

When most people in the church read about the thief on the cross, for instance, they immediately think of a burglar that held up a store or broke into a home. They may be rather shocked to find out that the guy was actually a Jewish revolutionary figure who was part of a growing movement in Palestine eager to throw off Roman rule.

It also comes as something of a surprise to contemporary Christians that "cursing" in the New Testament era had little or nothing to do with cussing somebody out. It had far more to do with the invocation of spirits to cause someone harm.

No doubt there is a need in the church for learning more about the world of the New Testament to avoid erroneous interpretations of the text of Scripture. But relevant historical and cultural insights also provide an added dimension of perspective to the words of the Bible. This kind of information often functions in the same way as watching a movie in color rather than in black and white. Finding out, for instance, how Paul compared Christ's victory on the cross to a joyous celebration parade in honor of a Roman general after winning an extraordinary battle brings does indeed magnify the profundity and implications of Jesus' work on the cross. Discovering that the factions at Corinth ("I follow Paul . . . I follow Apollos . . .") had plenty of precedent in the local cults ("I follow Aphrodite; I follow Apollo . . .") helps us understand the "why" of a particular problem. Learning about the water supply from the springs of Hierapolis that flowed into Laodicea as "lukewarm" water enables us to appreciate the relevance of the metaphor Jesus used when he addressed the spiritual laxity of this church.

My sense is that most Christians are eager to learn more about the real life setting of the New Testament. In the preaching and teaching of the Bible in the church, congregants are always grateful when they learn something of the background and historical context of the text. It not only helps them understand the text more accurately, but often enables them to identify with the people and circumstances of the Bible. I have been asked on countless occasions by Christians, "Where can I get access to good historical background information about this passage?" Earnest Christians are hungry for information that makes their Bibles come alive.

The stimulus for this commentary came from the church and the aim is to serve the church. The contributors to this series have sought to provide illuminating and interesting historical/cultural background information. The intent was to draw upon relevant papyri, inscriptions, archaeological discoveries, and the numerous studies of Judaism, Roman culture, Hellenism, and other features of the world of the New Testament and to make the results accessible to people in the church. We recognize that some readers of the commentary will want to go further, and so the sources of the information have been carefully documented in endnotes.

The written information has been supplemented with hundreds of photographs, maps, charts, artwork, and other graphics that help the reader better understand the world of the New Testament. Each of the writers was given an opportunity to dream up a "wish list" of illustrations that he thought would help to illustrate the passages in the New Testament book for which he was writing commentary. Although we were not able to obtain everything they were looking for, we came close.

The team of commentators are writing for the benefit of the broad array of Christians who simply want to better understand their Bibles from the vantage point of the historical context. This is an installment in a new genre of "Bible background" commentaries that was kicked off by Craig Keener's fine volume. Consequently, this is not an "exegetical" commentary that provides linguistic insight and background into Greek constructions and verb tenses. Neither is this work an "expository" commentary that provides a verse-by-verse exposition of the text; for in-depth philological or theological insight, readers will need to have other more specialized or comprehensive commentaries available. Nor is this an "historical-critical" commentary, although the contributors are all scholars and have already made substantial academic contributions on the New Testament books they are writing on for this set. The team intentionally does not engage all of the issues that are discussed in the scholarly guild.

Rather, our goal is to offer a reading and interpretation of the text informed by what we regard as the most relevant historical information. For many in the church, this commentary will serve as an important entry point into the interpretation and appreciation of the text. For other more serious students of the Word, these volumes will provide an important supplement to many of the fine exegetical, expository, and critical available.

The contributors represent a group of scholars who embrace the Bible as the Word of God and believe that the message of its pages has life-changing relevance for faith and practice today. Accordingly, we offer "Reflections" on the relevance of the Scripture to life for every chapter of the New Testament.

I pray that this commentary brings you both delight and insight in digging deeper into the Word of God.

Clinton E. Arnold
General Editor

LIST OF SIDEBARS

INDEX OF PHOTOS AND MAPS

ABBREVIATIONS

1. Books of the Bible and Apocrypha

1 Chron.	1 Chronicles	Josh.	Joshua
2 Chron.	2 Chronicles	Jude	Jude
1 Cor.	1 Corinthians	Judg.	Judges
2 Cor.	2 Corinthians	Judith	Judith
1 Esd.	1 Esdras	Lam.	Lamentations
2 Esd.	2 Esdras	Lev.	Leviticus
1 John	1 John	Luke	Luke
2 John	2 John	Mal.	Malachi
3 John	3 John	Mark	Mark
1 Kings	1 Kings	Matt.	Matthew
2 Kings	2 Kings	Mic.	Micah
1 Macc.	1 Maccabees	Nah.	Nahum
2 Macc.	2 Maccabees	Neh.	Nehemiah
1 Peter	1 Peter	Num.	Numbers
2 Peter	2 Peter	Obad.	Obadiah
1 Sam.	1 Samuel	Phil.	Philippians
2 Sam.	2 Samuel	Philem.	Philemon
1 Thess.	1 Thessalonians	Pr. Man.	Prayer of Manassah
2 Thess.	2 Thessalonians	Prov.	Proverbs
1 Tim.	1 Timothy	Ps.	Psalm
2 Tim.	2 Timothy	Rest. of Est.	The Rest of Esther
Acts	Acts	Rev.	Revelation
Amos	Amos	Rom.	Romans
Bar.	Baruch	Ruth	Ruth
Bel	Bel and the Dragon	S. of III Ch.	The Song of the Three Holy Children
Col.	Colossians	Sir.	Sirach/Ecclesiasticus
Dan.	Daniel	Song	Song of Songs
Deut.	Deuteronomy	Sus.	Susanna
Eccl.	Ecclesiastes	Titus	Titus
Ep. Jer.	Epistle of Jeremiah	Tobit	Tobit
Eph.	Ephesians	Wisd. Sol.	The Wisdom of Solomon
Est.	Esther	Zech.	Zechariah
Ezek.	Ezekiel	Zeph.	Zephaniah
Ex.	Exodus		
Ezra	Ezra		
Gal.	Galatians		
Gen.	Genesis		
Hab.	Habakkuk		
Hag.	Haggai		
Heb.	Hebrews		
Hos.	Hosea		
Isa.	Isaiah		
James	James		
Jer.	Jeremiah		
Job	Job		
Joel	Joel		
John	John		
Jonah	Jonah		

2. Old and New Testament Pseudepigrapha and Rabbinic Literature

Individual tractates of rabbinic literature follow the abbreviations of the *SBL Handbook of Style*, pp. 79–80. Qumran documents follow standard Dead Sea Scroll conventions.

2 Bar.	*2 Baruch*
3 Bar.	*3 Baruch*
4 Bar.	*4 Baruch*
1 En.	*1 Enoch*
2 En.	*2 Enoch*
3 En.	*3 Enoch*
4 Ezra	*4 Ezra*

3 Macc.	3 Maccabees
4 Macc.	4 Maccabees
5 Macc.	5 Maccabees
Acts Phil.	Acts of Philip
Acts Pet.	Acts of Peter and the 12 Apostles
Apoc. Elijah	Apocalypse of Elijah
As. Mos.	Assumption of Moses
b.	Babylonian Talmud (+ tractate)
Gos. Thom.	Gospel of Thomas
Jos. Asen.	Joseph and Aseneth
Jub.	Jubilees
Let. Aris.	Letter of Aristeas
m.	Mishnah (+ tractate)
Mek.	Mekilta
Midr.	Midrash I (+ biblical book)
Odes Sol.	Odes of Solomon
Pesiq. Rab.	Pesiqta Rabbati
Pirqe. R. El.	Pirqe Rabbi Eliezer
Pss. Sol.	Psalms of Solomon
Rab.	Rabbah (+biblical book); (e.g., Gen. Rab.=Genesis Rabbah)
S. ʿOlam Rab.	Seder ʿOlam Rabbah
Sem.	Semahot
Sib. Or.	Sibylline Oracles
T. Ab.	Testament of Abraham
T. Adam	Testament of Adam
T. Ash.	Testament of Asher
T. Benj.	Testament of Benjamin
T. Dan	Testament of Dan
T. Gad	Testament of Gad
T. Hez.	Testament of Hezekiah
T. Isaac	Testament of Isaac
T. Iss.	Testament of Issachar
T. Jac.	Testament of Jacob
T. Job	Testament of Job
T. Jos.	Testament of Joseph
T. Jud.	Testament of Judah
T. Levi	Testament of Levi
T. Mos.	Testament of Moses
T. Naph.	Testament of Naphtali
T. Reu.	Testament of Reuben
T. Sim.	Testament of Simeon
T. Sol.	Testament of Solomon
T. Zeb.	Testament of Zebulum
Tanh.	Tanhuma
Tg. Isa.	Targum of Isaiah
Tg. Lam.	Targum of Lamentations
Tg. Neof.	Targum Neofiti
Tg. Onq.	Targum Onqelos
Tg. Ps.-J	Targum Pseudo-Jonathan
y.	Jerusalem Talmud (+ tractate)

3. Classical Historians

For an extended list of classical historians and church fathers, see *SBL Handbook of Style*, pp. 84–

87. For many works of classical antiquity, the abbreviations have been subjected to the author's discretion; the names of these works should be obvious upon consulting entries of the classical writers in classical dictionaries or encyclopedias.

Eusebius

Eccl. Hist.	Ecclesiastical History

Josephus

Ag. Ap.	Against Apion
Ant.	Jewish Antiquities
J.W.	Jewish War
Life	The Life

Philo

Abraham	On the Life of Abraham
Agriculture	On Agriculture
Alleg. Interp	Allegorical Interpretation
Animals	Whether Animals Have Reason
Cherubim	On the Cherubim
Confusion	On the Confusion of Thomas
Contempl. Life	On the Contemplative Life
Creation	On the Creation of the World
Curses	On Curses
Decalogue	On the Decalogue
Dreams	On Dreams
Drunkenness	On Drunkenness
Embassy	On the Embassy to Gaius
Eternity	On the Eternity of the World
Flaccus	Against Flaccus
Flight	On Flight and Finding
Giants	On Giants
God	On God
Heir	Who Is the Heir?
Hypothetica	Hypothetica
Joseph	On the Life of Joseph
Migration	On the Migration of Abraham
Moses	On the Life of Moses
Names	On the Change of Names
Person	That Every Good Person Is Free
Planting	On Planting
Posterity	On the Posterity of Cain
Prelim. Studies	On the Preliminary Studies
Providence	On Providence
QE	Questions and Answers on Exodus
QG	Questions and Answers on Genesis
Rewards	On Rewards and Punishments
Sacrifices	On the Sacrifices of Cain and Abel
Sobriety	On Sobriety
Spec. Laws	On the Special Laws
Unchangeable	That God Is Unchangeable
Virtues	On the Virtues

Worse	*That the Worse Attacks the Better*

Apostolic Fathers

1 Clem.	*First Letter of Clement*
Barn.	*Epistle of Barnabas*
Clem. Hom.	*Ancient Homily of Clement (also called 2 Clement)*
Did.	*Didache*
Herm. Vis.; Sim.	*Shepherd of Hermas, Visions; Similitudes*
Ignatius	*Epistles of Ignatius (followed by the letter's name)*
Mart. Pol.	*Martyrdom of Polycarp*

4. Modern Abbreviations

AASOR	Annual of the American Schools of Oriental Research
AB	Anchor Bible
ABD	*Anchor Bible Dictionary*
ABRL	Anchor Bible Reference Library
AGJU	Arbeiten zur Geschichte des antiken Judentums und des Urchristentums
AH	*Agricultural History*
ALGHJ	Arbeiten zur Literatur und Geschichte des Hellenistischen Judentums
AnBib	Analecta biblica
ANRW	*Aufstieg und Niedergang der römischen Welt*
ANTC	Abingdon New Testament Commentaries
BAGD	Bauer, W., W. F. Arndt, F. W. Gingrich, and F. W. Danker. *Greek-English Lexicon of the New Testament and Other Early Christina Literature* (2d. ed.)
BA	*Biblical Archaeologist*
BAFCS	Book of Acts in Its First Century Setting
BAR	*Biblical Archaeology Review*
BASOR	*Bulletin of the American Schools of Oriental Research*
BBC	Bible Background Commentary
BBR	*Bulletin for Biblical Research*
BDB	Brown, F., S. R. Driver, and C. A. Briggs. *A Hebrew and English Lexicon of the Old Testament*
BDF	Blass, F., A. Debrunner, and R. W. Funk. *A Greek Grammar of the New Testament and Other Early Christian Literature*
BECNT	Baker Exegetical Commentary on the New Testament
BI	*Biblical Illustrator*
Bib	*Biblica*
BibSac	*Bibliotheca Sacra*
BLT	Brethren Life and Thought
BNTC	Black's New Testament Commentary
BRev	*Bible Review*
BSHJ	Baltimore Studies in the History of Judaism
BST	The Bible Speaks Today
BSV	Biblical Social Values
BT	*The Bible Translator*
BTB	*Biblical Theology Bulletin*
BZ	*Biblische Zeitschrift*
CBQ	*Catholic Biblical Quarterly*
CBTJ	*Calvary Baptist Theological Journal*
CGTC	Cambridge Greek Testament Commentary
CH	*Church History*
CIL	*Corpus inscriptionum latinarum*
CPJ	*Corpus papyrorum judaicorum*
CRINT	*Compendia rerum iudaicarum ad Novum Testamentum*
CTJ	*Calvin Theological Journal*
CTM	*Concordia Theological Monthly*
CTT	Contours of Christian Theology
DBI	*Dictionary of Biblical Imagery*
DCM	*Dictionary of Classical Mythology.*
DDD	*Dictionary of Deities and Demons in the Bible*
DJBP	*Dictionary of Judaism in the Biblical Period*
DJG	*Dictionary of Jesus and the Gospels*
DLNT	*Dictionary of the Later New Testament and Its Developments*
DNTB	*Dictionary of New Testament Background*
DPL	*Dictionary of Paul and His Letters*
EBC	*Expositor's Bible Commentary*
EDBT	*Evangelical Dictionary of Biblical Theology*
EDNT	*Exegetical Dictionary of the New Testament*
EJR	*Encyclopedia of the Jewish Religion*
EPRO	Études préliminaires aux religions orientales dans l'empire romain
EvQ	*Evangelical Quarterly*
ExpTim	*Expository Times*
FRLANT	Forsuchungen zur Religion und Literatur des Alten und Neuen Testament
GNC	Good News Commentary
GNS	Good News Studies
HCNT	*Hellenistic Commentary to the New Testament*
HDB	*Hastings Dictionary of the Bible*

HJP	History of the Jewish People in the Age of Jesus Christ, by E. Schürer	NEAE	New Encyclopedia of Archaeological Excavations in the Holy Land
HTR	Harvard Theological Review		
HTS	Harvard Theological Studies	NEASB	Near East Archaeological Society Bulletin
HUCA	Hebrew Union College Annual		
IBD	Illustrated Bible Dictionary	New Docs	New Documents Illustrating Early Christianity
IBS	Irish Biblical Studies		
ICC	International Critical Commentary	NIBC	New International Biblical Commentary
IDB	The Interpreter's Dictionary of the Bible	NICNT	New International Commentary on the New Testament
IEJ	Israel Exploration Journal	NIDNTT	New International Dictionary of New Testament Theology
IG	Inscriptiones graecae		
IGRR	Inscriptiones graecae ad res romanas pertinentes	NIGTC	New International Greek Testament Commentary
ILS	Inscriptiones Latinae Selectae	NIVAC	NIV Application Commentary
Imm	Immanuel	NorTT	Norsk Teologisk Tidsskrift
ISBE	International Standard Bible Encyclopedia	NoT	Notes on Translation
		NovT	Novum Testamentum
Int	Interpretation	NovTSup	Novum Testamentum Supplements
IvE	Inschriften von Ephesos		
IVPNTC	InterVarsity Press New Testament Commentary	NTAbh	Neutestamentliche Abhandlungen
JAC	Jahrbuch fur Antike und Christentum	NTS	New Testament Studies
		NTT	New Testament Theology
JBL	Journal of Biblical Literature	NTTS	New Testament Tools and Studies
JETS	Journal of the Evangelical Theological Society		
		OAG	Oxford Archaeological Guides
JHS	Journal of Hellenic Studies	OCCC	Oxford Companion to Classical Civilization
JJS	Journal of Jewish Studies		
JOAIW	Jahreshefte des Osterreeichischen Archaologischen Instites in Wien	OCD	Oxford Classical Dictionary
		ODCC	The Oxford Dictionary of the Christian Church
JSJ	Journal for the Study of Judaism in the Persian, Hellenistic, and Roman Periods		
		OGIS	Orientis graeci inscriptiones selectae
JRS	Journal of Roman Studies	OHCW	The Oxford History of the Classical World
JSNT	Journal for the Study of the New Testament		
		OHRW	Oxford History of the Roman World
JSNTSup	Journal for the Study of the New Testament: Supplement Series	OTP	Old Testament Pseudepigrapha, ed. by J. H. Charlesworth
JSOT	Journal for the Study of the Old Testament		
JSOTSup	Journal for the Study of the Old Testament: Supplement Series	PEQ	Palestine Exploration Quarterly
		PG	Patrologia graeca
JTS	Journal of Theological Studies	PGM	Papyri graecae magicae: Die griechischen Zauberpapyri
KTR	Kings Theological Review		
LCL	Loeb Classical Library	PL	Patrologia latina
LEC	Library of Early Christianity	PNTC	Pelican New Testament Commentaries
LSJ	Liddell, H. G., R. Scott, H. S. Jones. A Greek-English Lexicon		
		Rb	Revista biblica
MM	Moulton, J. H., and G. Milligan. The Vocabulary of the Greek Testament	RB	Revue biblique
		RivB	Rivista biblica italiana
		RTR	Reformed Theological Review
MNTC	Moffatt New Testament Commentary	SB	Sources bibliques
		SBL	Society of Biblical Literature
NBD	New Bible Dictionary	SBLDS	Society of Biblical Literature Dissertation Series
NC	Narrative Commentaries		
NCBC	New Century Bible Commentary Eerdmans	SBLMS	Society of Biblical Literature Monograph Series

SBLSP	*Society of Biblical Literature Seminar Papers*
SBS	Stuttgarter Bibelstudien
SBT	Studies in Biblical Theology
SCJ	*Stone-Campbell Journal*
Scr	*Scripture*
SE	*Studia Evangelica*
SEG	*Supplementum epigraphicum graecum*
SJLA	Studies in Judaism in Late Antiquity
SJT	*Scottish Journal of Theology*
SNTSMS	Society for New Testament Studies Monograph Series
SSC	Social Science Commentary
SSCSSG	Social-Science Commentary on the Synoptic Gospels
Str-B	Strack, H. L., and P. Billerbeck. *Kommentar zum Neuen Testament aus Talmud und Midrasch*
TC	Thornapple Commentaries
TDNT	*Theological Dictionary of the New Testament*
TDOT	*Theological Dictionary of the Old Testament*
TLNT	*Theological Lexicon of the New Testament*
TLZ	*Theologische Literaturzeitung*
TNTC	Tyndale New Testament Commentary
TrinJ	*Trinity Journal*
TS	*Theological Studies*
TSAJ	Texte und Studien zum antiken Judentum
TWNT	*Theologische Wörterbuch zum Neuen Testament*
TynBul	*Tyndale Bulletin*
WBC	Word Biblical Commentary Waco: Word, 1982

WMANT	Wissenschaftliche Monographien zum Alten und Neuen Testament
WUNT	Wissenschaftliche Untersuchungen zum Neuen Testament
YJS	Yale Judaica Series
ZNW	*Zeitschrift fur die neutestamentliche Wissenschaft und die Junde der alteren Kirche*
ZPE	*Zeischrift der Papyrolgie und Epigraphkik*
ZPEB	*Zondervan Pictorial Encyclopedia of the Bible*

5. General Abbreviations

ad. loc.	in the place cited
b.	born
c., ca.	circa
cf.	compare
d.	died
ed(s).	editors(s), edited by
e.g.	for example
ET	English translation
frg.	fragment
i.e.	that is
ibid.	in the same place
idem	the same (author)
lit.	literally
l(l)	line(s)
MSS	manuscripts
n.d.	no date
NS	New Series
par.	parallel
passim	here and there
repr.	reprint
ser.	series
s.v.	*sub verbo,* under the word
trans.	translator, translated by; transitive

Zondervan Illustrated Bible Backgrounds Commentary

1 THESSALONIANS

by Jeffrey A. D. Weima

The City of Thessalonica

A noble history. Cassander, a former general of Alexander the Great and later king of Macedonia, founded the city of Thessalonica in 315 B.C. He named the new community after his wife, the half sister of Alexander. The city was captured in 167 B.C. by the Romans and made the capital of one of their four newly created districts in this region. When the Romans reorganized these four districts into a single province in 146 B.C., Thessalonica was designated as the capital city. Just over a century later in 42 B.C., the city was rewarded for helping the victorious Mark Antony and Octavian in the Roman civil wars by being made a "free city." This favored status resulted in such privileges as a measure of autonomy over local affairs, the right to mint its own coins, freedom from military occupation, and certain tax concessions.

NEAPOLIS, MACEDONIA

The modern harbor of the city where Paul arrived in Macedonia.

▶ **1 Thessalonians**
IMPORTANT FACTS:

- **AUTHOR:** Paul (despite his mentioning Silas and Timothy as cosenders).
- **DATE:** A.D. 51 (Paul writes from Corinth).
- **PURPOSES:**
  - To defend the integrity of Paul.
  - To encourage the church to endure persecution.
  - To exhort the church to live holy lives.
  - To comfort and teach the church about Christ's return.

A strategic location. Two geographical factors resulted in Thessalonica's quickly becoming the most populous (100,000 people), wealthy, and thus important city in Macedonia.[1] First, the city possessed a natural harbor that was the best in the entire Aegean Sea. Second, the city was located on the juncture of the Via Egnatia (the major east-west highway that extended from Asia Minor all the way to Rome) and the road north to Danube. Thessalonica was thus ideally situated for both commercial and military enterprises. As Meletius observed so many years ago: "So long as nature does not change, Thessalonica will remain wealthy and fortunate."[2]

A unique political structure. Thessalonica, as a free city, was allowed to keep its traditional structure of a democratic civil administration, unlike its neighboring communities. The lowest level involved a citizen assembly that handled public business. The Jews initially attempted to bring Paul and Silas before this assembly (Acts 17:5). The higher level of administration involved the city council, which consisted of five or six local authorities called "politarchs" (the NIV simply refers to them as "city officials"), the city treasurer, and the gymnasiarch. The Jews, after enlisting the aid of certain disreputable men, seized Jason and some other converts and brought them not to the citizen assembly but to the politarchs (17:6–8).

A religiously pluralistic environment. Like other major urban centers in the ancient world, Thessalonica had plenty of religious competitors to the Christ proclaimed by Paul.[3] A religiously pluralistic environment is indicated by the apostle's words that the majority of the Thessalonian believers had "turned to God from idols" (1 Thess. 1:9). Archaeological and inscriptural evidence also reveals the popularity of various mystery religions dedicated to such Greco-Roman and Egyptian deities as Dionysius, Serapis, Isis, Aphrodite, Demeter, Zeus, and Asclepius. The most important deity in Thessalonica, however, was Cabirus—the

▶ Politarchs

The office of politarch, mentioned twice by Luke in his description of Paul's ministry in Thessalonica (Acts 17:6, 8), is unique to the province of Macedonia and found only rarely in other cities. Archaeologists have so far discovered twenty-eight references to this distinctive office in Thessalonica.[A-1] These findings prove that Luke was familiar with the political structure of the different cities in Paul's journeys and thus suggest that his recording of these travels in Acts is historically reliable.

patron god of the city. This Cabirus figure was a martyred hero, murdered by his two brothers, buried with symbols of royal power, and expected to return to help the oppressed poor in general and the citizens of Thessalonica in particular. It has been suggested that similarities between Cabirus and the story of Jesus account for the success of Paul's ministry in this city.[4]

The diverse religious context of Thessalonica included a Jewish synagogue. The size and influence of this synagogue are suggested by the presence of "a large number of God-fearing Greeks" (Gentiles who converted to Judaism but who did not allow themselves to be circumcised) as well as "not a few prominent women" (Acts 17:4).

The imperial cult with its worship of Rome and the emperor also played a key role in the religious life of Thessalonica. On the one hand, the imperial cult served to ensure the ongoing favor of the current Roman emperor by visibly demonstrating the city's allegiance to his leadership. On the other hand, the imperial cult also helped to sustain Roman rule over the local populace by stressing the divine nature of the emperors as well as the benefits the city enjoyed under their rule. In this political and religious context, it is not surprising that Paul's preaching about "another king . . . Jesus" would alarm civic sensibilities and lead to the accusation that he was violating "Caesar's decrees" (Acts 17:7). Similarly, the failure of the Thessalonian believers to continue to participate in the imperial cult and in the worship of other pagan deities aroused the anger of their fellow citizens and quickly led to the persecution of this newly planted church.

Paul and the Thessalonian Church

Philippi to Thessalonica. Paul's relationship with the Thessalonian church began during the middle of his second missionary

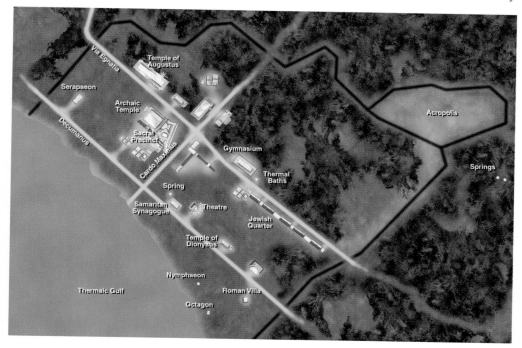

journey. The apostle, along with Silas and Timothy, departed from Philippi, leaving Luke behind to pastor the newly founded church there. This small group of missionaries traveled some ninety miles along the Via Egnatia, passing through two cities of lesser importance, Amphipolis and Apollonia, and arriving on the third day in Thessalonica (Acts 17:1; 1 Thess. 2:1–2).

Thessalonica. Paul began his evangelistic activity in the local synagogue, where he preached for three Sabbaths. This resulted in the conversion of some Jews and even more Gentiles, including a number of wealthy women from leading families in the community (Acts 17:2–4). These Gentiles had earlier been attracted to Judaism but now underwent a second conversion to Christianity. During the rest of the week, Paul and his co-missionaries supported themselves by working as tentmakers (cf. 18:3). In this way, they not only provided the church with a good example of proper conduct in the area of work but also avoided any potential charges that they preached the gospel only to win followers and to obtain financial gain (1 Thess. 2:9; 2 Thess. 3:7).

It is commonly assumed that Paul won converts by preaching in the marketplaces ("street corner" evangelism). Nevertheless, there is good evidence that

his missionary work took place in the workshop and the private home.[5] We can picture the apostle in Thessalonica laboring in a local workshop, perhaps one owned by Jason (Acts 17:5). During the long hours at his workbench, cutting and sewing leather to make tents, Paul would have had opportunities to share the gospel with fellow workers, customers, and other citizens who were interested in this tentmaker-philosopher newly arrived in the city. Those who wanted to know more about Paul and his message would have returned for individual instruction (1 Thess. 2:11, lit., "we exhorted *each one of you*"), either in the workshop or a believer's private home. Many accepted Paul's message as the word of God (2:13) and so turned from idols to serve the living God (1:9). These Gentile converts from paganism soon made up the major-

right ▶

THE LION OF AMPHIPOLIS

A thirty-foot high stone monument along the *Via Egnatia*.

MACEDONIA
▼

ity of the believers in the Thessalonian church.

Paul's success, however, quickly aroused opposition. The synagogue leaders were upset by the loss of its members and the city officials were similarly alarmed by the conversion of its wealthy women to a cult that worshiped an alternate emperor. The unbelieving Jews acted first and, with the help of some troublemakers, managed to start a city riot against the infant church. The crowd originally intended to bring Paul, Silas, and Timothy to the lowest level of administration: the popular assembly (Acts 17:5). But when they could not find the missionaries, they instead seized Jason, their host, and a few other congregational members and brought them to the higher officials: the politarchs (17:6). Two charges—one general, the other specific—were laid against the missionaries in absentia: first, they were disturbing the peace; second, they had violated the decrees of Caesar (17:7).

Thessalonica to Berea. In order to protect Jason and the other converts, Paul and his two traveling companions had no option but to leave quietly in the middle of the night. They traveled for two or three days southwest to Berea (Acts 17:10). Here, in sharp contrast to the hostility of the Jews in Thessalonica, Paul received a warm reception from his countrymen (17:11).

Berea to Athens. The peaceful ministry setting of Berea was soon disturbed by Thessalonian Jews who once again forced Paul to leave town in a hurry. The apostle was escorted by some believers all the way to Athens, likely traveling by road to the port city of Dion and by sea the remainder of the journey. Silas and Timothy stayed behind briefly in Berea, rejoining Paul in Athens shortly thereafter (Acts 17:13–15; 1 Thess. 3:1–2).

Athens. During his stay in Athens, Paul continued to worry about his young converts in Thessalonica and the persecution they were enduring. Therefore, he sent Timothy back to Thessalonica (1 Thess. 3:1–5) and Silas possibly to Philippi. Paul dearly wanted to revisit the Thessalonians himself but was prevented from doing so (2:18).

Athens to Corinth. After a frustrating ministry in Athens, Paul arrived in Corinth for an eighteen-month stay. Timothy and Silas rejoined Paul after their trip to Macedonia (Acts 18:5), apparently with donated funds from the Thessalonian and Philippian churches, which allowed the apostle to quit his tent-making work and preach full time. Timothy gave Paul an initially good report about the Thessalonian church but also informed him of a few problems (1 Thess. 3:6–10). This news caused Paul to write his first letter to the church in A.D. 51. A short time later the apostle received an alarming report about the spread of a false teaching to the effect that "the day of the Lord has already come" (2 Thess. 2:2), as well as a reoccurrence of the problem of believers who refused to work. Paul, therefore, felt the need to write to the Thessalonian church for a second time.

Later visits to Thessalonica. Paul had ongoing contact with the believers in Thessalonica in his later years of ministry. He visited them twice on his third missionary journey, both on his way to Corinth via Macedonia (Acts 19:21) and on his way back from that city (20:1–6).

He may have also visited them during his fourth missionary journey, following his prison journey to Rome and subsequent release. That Paul enjoyed good relations with the Thessalonian church in the years after his two letters to them is clear from the fact that they contributed to the collection he was gathering for the needy churches in Palestine (Rom.15:26; 2 Cor. 8:1–5; 9:4) and also apparently supported him in his own evangelistic work (2 Cor. 11:9).

Why Did Paul Write 1 Thessalonians?

After Timothy returned from his second visit to Thessalonica, he gave Paul an essentially good report about the spiritual health of the young church (1 Thess. 3:6–9). Yet, Timothy also informed the apostle about some concerns that caused Paul to write 1 Thessalonians:

Concern about Paul's integrity: Non-Christians in Thessalonica (1 Thess. 2:14, "your own countrymen") accused Paul of having impure, selfish motives. Paul, therefore, spends much of the first half of the letter defending himself, first for his past conduct in their midst (2:1–16), and second for his present inability to revisit them (2:17–3:10).

Concern about persecution: The Thessalonian Christians not only accepted the gospel "in spite of severe suffering" (1 Thess. 1:6), they also continued to endure opposition for their faith after their conversion.[6] Paul, therefore, seeks to encourage his persecuted readers.

Concern about proper conduct: When the Thessalonian Christians "turned . . . from idols to serve the living and true God" (1 Thess. 1:9), their conversion involved a radically different lifestyle. Paul, therefore, emphasizes throughout the letter, but especially in the second half (4:1–5:22), the Thessalonians' need to live a holy or sanctified life.

Concern about Christ's Return: The Thessalonian Christians had questions concerning the fate of believers who die before Jesus' second coming (1 Thess. 4:13–18) as well as the "times and dates" of Christ's return (5:1–11). Paul, therefore, writes 1 Thessalonians in order to clarify these and other matters connected with Christ's return.

Letter Opening (1:1)

The opening section of letters in the ancient world follows a fixed pattern consisting of three elements: the sender, the recipient, and the greeting. It is clear that Paul has been influenced by this pattern as he begins his first letter to the Thessalonians with the same three elements in their expected order. But

VIA EGNATIA
▼

instead of slavishly following the episto-lary custom of his day, Paul has "Christianized" somewhat his letter opening. He takes the typical Greek greeting *chairein* ("Greetings!") and replaces it with the similar sounding word *charis* ("grace"). The apostle also adds to this salutation the typical Jewish welcome of "peace," thereby creating a distinctively Christian greeting ("Grace and peace to you") that honors both Gentile and Jewish believer alike.

Paul, Silas and Timothy (1:1). Paul differs from the typical letter opening of his day by including as cosenders the names of others who were with him. This, along with the frequent use of the plural "we" throughout the letter, has led some to conclude that 1 Thessalonians was written by all three of the individuals named in the letter opening. The use of the first person "I" (2:18; 3:5; 5:27), however, reveals that Paul is the real author of this letter. The names of Silas and Timothy are included because of their substantial role in the establishment and later support of the Thessalonian church.

Thanksgiving (1:2–10)

Paul's letters typically include a thanksgiving that is located after the letter opening and before the letter body. This part of the letter is called a "thanksgiving" because of the main verb that introduces this section ("I/We give thanks. . .") as well as its general content: thanksgiving to God for the believers to whom Paul is writing.

Some ancient letters similarly open with a brief thanksgiving to the gods. For example, this third century B.C. letter begins: "Toubias to Apollonios, greeting. If you are well and if all your affairs and everything else is proceeding according

to your will, many thanks to the gods."[7] Paul's thanksgivings, however, differ from such ancient letters in that his deal with the spiritual rather than the physical well-being of his recipients and are much longer and formally complex.

The Pauline thanksgiving possesses at least three important functions. First, it has a *pastoral* function: The thanksgiving reestablishes the apostle's relationship with his readers by means of a positive expression of gratitude to God for their faith and work. This is important if Paul wants his letters to be accepted and his exhortations to be obeyed by his readers. Second, it has a *paraenetic* function: There is an implicit (or even, at times, explicit) challenge for the readers to live up to the praise that the apostle is giving them in his words of thanksgiving. Third, the thanksgiving has a *foreshadowing* function: It anticipates the main themes to be developed in the body of the letter.[8]

Your work produced by faith, your labor prompted by love, and your endurance inspired by hope (1:3). The first or immediate reason why Paul gives thanks to God focuses on three things that the Thessalonian Christians are doing. The first is "your work produced by faith." Although Paul was vehemently opposed to "legalism"—the belief that salvation

comes through the works of the law—he was by no means antinomistic (i.e., against the law). This allows him to pair the words "work" and "faith" together to refer to that Christian activity that results from faith—what Paul elsewhere refers to as "faith expressing itself through love" (Gal. 5:6). The second phrase, "your labor prompted by love," somewhat similarly refers to those Christian deeds that stem from love. The third phrase, "your endurance inspired by hope," refers to the hope that the Thessalonians continue to have in the imminent return of Christ.

He has chosen you (1:4). The second or ultimate reason why Paul gives thanks shifts the focus from what the Thessalonian Christians are doing to what God has done: "He has chosen you." The Greek phrase literally means "your election" and ought to be interpreted in light of the language elsewhere in the letter of God's "calling" and "appointing" the Thessalonians (2:12; 4:7; 5:9, 24). By identifying his readers as God's elect, Paul applies language reserved exclusively for Israel to the predominantly Gentile church in Thessalonica. The fact that the apostle uses the term *election* without any accompanying explanation suggests that this subject must have been an integral part of his original preaching in the Thessalonian church.

Because our gospel came to you (1:5). The apologetic reference to Paul's original preaching ministry in Thessalonica in 1:5a ("because our gospel came to you not simply with words, but also with power, with the Holy Spirit and with deep conviction") as well as the defense of his integrity in 1:5b ("You know how we lived among you for your sake") foreshadows the lengthy defense of his

integrity in 2:1–16. The honest and sincere character of the apostle should be evident to the Thessalonians, first in his powerful and passionate preaching, which was likely accompanied by miracles and second, in the personal knowledge they have of how he acted in their midst.[9]

You became imitators of us and of the Lord (1:6). The individualism that characterizes our modern society might easily lead to the notion that imitating another person involves the denial of one's true and unique identity such that he or she is really a "phony." In the ancient world, however, the idea of imitating others was common.[10] Thus, not only is Paul following a widespread practice of his day but his failure to make use of the imitation theme may have opened himself up to charges that he considered himself an unworthy teacher for his followers to emulate.

In spite of severe suffering (1:6). The reference here and elsewhere to the suffering experienced by the Thessalonian church does not likely refer to physical persecution but to social harassment.[11] There is virtually no evidence that Christians anywhere in the Roman empire during the 50s suffered from any organized opposition or physical oppression. Many sources do indicate, however, the offense, even disgust, felt by non-Christian neighbors and fellow citizens when converts to Christianity declined to take part in normal social and cultic activities (see "Social Harassment of Christians in the Greco-Roman World").[12]

The Lord's message rang out (1:8). Paul uses the rare verb *exēcheō* here, from which the English word "echo" is ultimately derived. The image that the apostle presents is that of a sound—the gospel message—that emanates from the Thessalonian Christians and echoes throughout the hills and valleys of Macedonia, Achaia, and beyond.

How you turned to God from idols (1:9). A variety of pagan deities were worshiped in Thessalonica. Archaeologists have discovered a temple dedicated to the Egyptian god Serapis, where a board of some fourteen priests ensured that the rites of the Nile were performed diligently. Inscriptions unearthed from this temple indicate that the Egyptian goddess Isis, who is associated with culture and mysteries, was also worshiped here. Epigraphic evidence reveals that Dionysus, the god of wine and joy, was among the more influential religious cults in Thessalonica. The patron god of the city, however, was Cabirus, about whom unfortunately little is known (see the Introduction). Other gods worshiped

in Thessalonica included Aphrodite, Demeter, Zeus, and Asclepius. The ceremonies associated with these diverse cults offered regeneration, immortality, a measure of equality and self-respect for an initiate, relief from ills and misfortune, and the promise of sexual fulfillment—concerns addressed to some degree in Paul's two letters to the Thessalonians.[13]

To wait for his Son from heaven (1:10). The eschatological subjects of Christ's return in 1:10a ("to wait for his Son from heaven") and the final judgment in 1:10b ("who rescues us from the coming wrath") anticipate well the discussion of these matters in 4:13–18 and 5:1–11.

Defense of Paul's Past Visit to Thessalonica (2:1–16)

The central theme of 2:1–16 is a defense of Paul's integrity during his past visit to Thessalonica. That this defense of his integrity was a major concern to the apostle is clear from the fact that it is the first topic he chooses to take up in the body of the letter. The importance of this subject is also evident from the way in which he foreshadowed his defensive concern in the thanksgiving (see comments on 1:5).

From whom is Paul defending himself? Paul's opponents come from *outside* the church. The good report of Timothy about the congregation (3:6), the exemplary character of the Thessalonian believers' life (1:6–7), Paul's description of them as "our glory and joy" at Christ's return (2:19–20), and his frequent reference to them as "brothers"(1:4; 2:1, 9, 14, 17; 3:7; 4:1, 13; 5:1, 4, 12, 14, 25) make it impossible to conclude that Paul was facing attack from believers inside the church. The best candidate for opponents

REFLECTIONS

THE THESSALONIAN CHRISTIANS exemplify a healthy balance between ethics and eschatology. Some contemporary believers emphasize only serving God in the present and so fail to anticipate the glorious return of Christ in the future. Others today stress the Second Coming so much that they devote little thought or energy to serving God in this world. In contrast, the Thessalonians' passion for serving God and so living a holy life in the present (1:9) is matched by their fervent hope in the future and glorious return of Christ (1:10).

outside the church are "your own countrymen"(2:14): unbelieving citizens of Thessalonica who not only persecuted the church but also attacked the church's leader, Paul, who was, in their minds, the source of the problem.

What were the charges brought against Paul? A careful reading of 2:1–16 reveals that Paul is defending himself against attacks on his integrity and the genuineness of his motives. Non-Christians in Thessalonica accused Paul of being no different than other wandering philosopher-teachers of his day: those who taught and spoke only to receive money and praise. There are enough clues available to see how unbelievers in Thessalonica opposed to this new religious movement founded by Paul might "spin" certain facts in a way in which the apostle's integrity would be questioned. The fact that Paul received money at least twice from the Philippian church during his original ministry in Thessalonica (Phil. 4:16), the fact that Paul converted among others in Thessalonica "not a few prominent [i.e., wealthy] women" (Acts 17:4) as well as Jason, who was rich enough to host the missionaries and post bond for them (17:5–9), the fact that Paul abruptly left the Thessalonian church, leaving them "orphaned" (see 1 Thess. 2:17) and has not yet returned to Thessalonica or, prior to this letter, even written them (3:1–6)—all this information could easily be used by opponents of the Thessalonian church to question the integrity of its founder.[14]

Our visit to you was not a failure (2:1). The NIV's translation of *kenē* as "failure" is better rendered here as "insincere." Paul, then, is defending the honesty of his motives during his past visit rather than the positive results of that visit.

Nor are we trying to trick you (2:3). The word "trick" (*dolos*) originally referred to catching fish by means of a bait and so developed the metaphorical meaning of "deceit, cunning, treachery."[15] Paul claims that he used no dishonest means to trick people into believing his preaching. The apostle's conduct, therefore, differs sharply from that of wandering philosopher-teachers, who employed various methods of deception to win followers and financial gain.[16]

We were gentle among you (2:7a). Instead of the word "gentle" (*ēpioi*) found in the NIV, more ancient and reliable manuscripts have the word "infants" (*nēpioi*), so that a better translation of this text reads: "We became *infants* among you."[17] This is the first of three striking family metaphors that Paul uses in this passage: "infants" (2:7a), "mother" (2:7b), and "father" (2:11). The purpose of this first metaphor of infants is to highlight the apostle's integrity. Unlike the wandering philosopher-teachers of that day, who were only interested in "pleas[ing] men" and who "used flattery" as a "mask to cover up greed" (2:4–5), Paul and his fellow missionaries acted as innocent as infants. Philo similarly speaks about the innocence of infants, claiming that "it is impossible for the greatest liar to invent a charge against them, as they are wholly innocent" (*Special Laws* 3.119).

Like a mother (2:7b). Instead of the common word for "mother" (*mētēr*), Paul employs a term with the specialized meaning of "wet nurse" (*trophos*), someone who suckles children. The use of wet nurses was widespread in the Greco-Roman world, and ancient writers typically portrayed the wet nurse as an important and beloved figure.[18] Since the original text refers to this woman nursing her *own* children, Paul has in view here the natural mother rather than the hired wet nurse. Yet he uses the unusual term *trophos* because this metaphor of a nursing mother underscores his sincere love for the Thessalonian Christians. A hired nurse competently cares for the children in her charge, but she cherishes her own children even more.

We loved you so much (2:8). The meaning of the rare verb used here (*homeiromai*) is illuminated by a fourth-century A.D. tombstone inscription (*CIG* 3.4000.7), where the term describes a father and mother's sad yearning for their deceased child. The word, therefore, expresses the deep affection that Paul has for the Thessalonian Christians, an affection like that between a parent and child.

We worked night and day (2:9). Although Paul does not say what kind of work he did, there are hints at his profession. He and his colleagues worked "with our own hands" (1 Cor. 4:12; cf. Acts 20:34), probably as tentmakers (Acts 18:3). Since tents were usually made with leather, it may be better to call Paul a "leather worker," one who not only made and repaired tents but a range of leather goods.[19] Paul likely learned this trade as part of his rabbinical training, since Jewish teachers were expected to support themselves by some form of labor.[20]

As a father (2:11). Paul likens himself to a father when he wants to emphasize the nurturing or instructional role he played in the lives of his converts.[21] The father in the Greco-Roman world was normally responsible for the education and training of his children.

The Jews, who . . . (2:14–16). The strong language that Paul uses in these verses to describe the Jews has led some to claim that this text is anti-Semitic and cannot have come from the hand of the apostle but is instead an addition inserted in the letter by a later writer.[22] Although the language is admittedly harsh, it stems from Paul's frustration with fellow Jews whose behavior has threatened the Gentile mission. The apostle does not have in view all Jews but only those who in some way were involved in the events mentioned in verses 15–16.[23] Furthermore, Paul speaks here somewhat hyperbolically as he also does elsewhere in his writings.[24]

The wrath of God has come upon them at last (2:16). There are a number of national disasters that the Jews suffered to which Paul may be referring: e.g., the famine in A.D. 46 (Acts 11:28), the banishment from Rome in A.D. 49 (Acts 18:2), persecutions under Tiberius Alexander.[25] It is also possible, however,

REFLECTIONS

NON-CHRISTIANS OFTEN DISMISS the claims of the gospel by pointing to the lack of integrity that many believers exemplify. They are especially quick to ridicule those disgraced TV evangelists who have preached the gospel only out of the selfish desire for human praise or financial gain. Believers today, therefore, must uphold the integrity of the gospel by following the example of Paul during his original visit to Thessalonica: He was as innocent as an infant (2:7b), as loving as a nursing mother (2:7c), and as nurturing as a father (2:11).

that the apostle is writing about an imminent judgment rather than a past one.[26]

Defense of Paul's Present Absence from Thessalonica (2:17–3:10)

The unbelieving citizens of Thessalonica (2:14) not only attacked the integrity of Paul with respect to his past visit to the city (2:1–16) but apparently also used the apostle's inability thus far to come back to the fledgling church to cast further doubts about the genuineness of his motives. One key concern of Paul in this section of the letter, therefore, is to reassure the Thessalonian Christians of his continued love and concern for them, despite his present failure to return for a second visit.

A second key concern focuses on the suffering that the Thessalonians are enduring for their commitment to Christ. Paul wants to encourage them to remain steadfast in their newfound faith even in the face of opposition. Although this second concern about persecution differs rather greatly from the first concern about Paul's separation from the Thessalonians, there is a link that logically connects these two topics together: Paul's original departure from Thessalonica and his inability to return were both the result of the same persecution that the believers in that city are currently experiencing.

Therefore, despite the differing themes that are addressed, 2:17–3:10 follows a logical line of argumentation. Paul begins with the first concern of his separation from the Thessalonians in 2:17–20. He then addresses the second concern of persecution in 3:1–5. The apostle concludes his argument by bringing the two concerns together in the good report about the Thessalonians given by the returning Timothy in 3:6–10.

We were torn away from you (2:17). The verb *aporphanizō* literally means "to be orphaned." The apostle thus depicts himself as a parent who has been orphaned from his children. This orphan metaphor conveys to the believers in Thessalonica Paul's feelings of deep anguish because of his separation from them.

Satan stopped us (2:18). The verb *enkoptō*, which literally means "to cut into," originally referred to the military practice of cutting up a road so as to make it impassable for a pursuing army.[27] Paul wants his readers to know that his present absence from them is not due to his personal choice but to the activity of Satan, who, in typical military fashion, has destroyed the apostle's path back to Thessalonica.

The crown in which we will glory (2:19). The crown that Paul refers to is not a royal tiara but a laurel wreath given to the victor in a Greek athletic contest. These crowns were woven out of palm or other branches, flowers, or certain plant

REFLECTIONS

PAUL STRESSES THAT PERSECUTION FOR ONE'S FAITH in Christ is a normal and expected feature of the Christian life (3:3b–4). There are many Christians in the world—brothers and sisters in such places as Laos, Saudi Arabia, Iraq, Sudan, Pakistan, Indonesia, and China (to mention only some)—who experience this truth every day in the form of church burnings or closings, harassment, fines, arrest, and imprisonment. Although believers in North America and elsewhere enjoy a certain measure of freedom and protection, they too ought to expect and be willing to be ridiculed and oppressed for their commitment to Christ.[A-2]

life.[28] Such crowns or wreaths would thus soon deteriorate—unlike the imperishable and unfading crown given to believers (1 Cor. 9:25; 1 Pet. 5:4). Paul encourages the Christians in Thessalonica by confidently claiming that they will be his victory wreath at the return of Christ.

We/I could stand it no longer (3:1, 5). Paul twice uses the uncommon verb *stegō*, which originally referred to keeping water out of a vessel, such as with a watertight house or a boat that doesn't leak.[29] The image that the apostle paints, therefore, is of his deep affection for the Thessalonians that he is no longer able to contain within himself and prevent from leaking out.

But Timothy . . . has brought good news about your faith and love (3:6). Timothy returns from Thessalonica with a good report that takes up the two concerns raised earlier in this passage. Paul's first concern about his separation from the Thessalonians (2:17–20) is answered with the news of the church's "love" for him: "that you always have pleasant memories of us and that you long to see us" (3:6). Paul's second concern about the persecution that his converts are enduring (3:1–5) is answered with the news of the church's "faith": that "in all our distress and persecution we were encouraged about you because of your faith . . . since you are standing firm in the Lord" (3:7–8).

◀ *left*

ATHLETE WITH WREATHS

A stone relief from Isthmia depicting a victorious athlete with his crowns.

▶ Who Went Where and What Did They Do?

A comparison of the movements of Paul and his coworkers described in 1 Thessalonians 3:1–10 with the account in Acts suggests that the following sequence of events likely took place:

Paul arrives in Athens (1 Thess. 3:1; see Acts 17:15–34), having left Silas and Timothy behind in Berea with instructions to rejoin him "as soon as possible" (Acts 17:15b).

After his two coworkers return to him in Athens, Paul sends Timothy back to Thessalonica in order to encourage the church that was being persecuted for its newfound faith (3:1–5).

Paul sends Silas somewhere in Macedonia (Acts 18:5), perhaps to the Philippian church, from which he received financial gifts to support the apostle and his coworkers in their preaching ministry (see Phil. 1:4; 4:10–20).

Silas and Timothy return to Paul (1 Thess. 3:6; see Acts 18:5), who by this time has left Athens to begin an eighteen-month ministry in Corinth (Acts 18:1–17).

Timothy gives an essentially good report about the Thessalonian church (3:6–10) but also informs Paul of several concerns, thereby prompting the apostle to write 1 Thessalonians.

Transitionary Prayers (3:11–13)

Paul moves from the first half of the letter body (2:1–3:10) to the second half (4:1–5:22) by means of two prayers (3:11–13).[30] The first prayer that God "may . . . clear the way for us to come to you" (3:11) looks back to Paul's concern in the previous verses about his separation from the Thessalonians (2:17–3:10). The second prayer looks ahead to three concerns that Paul is about to address: "so that you will be blameless and holy" (3:13) foreshadows the discussion of holiness in sexual conduct in 4:3–8; "make your love increase and overflow"(3:12) anticipates the discussion of brotherly love in 4:9–12; and "when our Lord Jesus comes" (3:13) prefigures the discussion of the return of Christ in 4:13–5:11.

Now may our God and Father himself and our Lord Jesus (3:11). The fact that the plural subjects of "God" and "Lord Jesus" occur with a singular form of the verb may suggest that Paul views these

two as essentially a unity and so affirms the full deity of Jesus.[31] The close collocation of God and Jesus in the prayer indicates minimally that the apostle sees the two working together in unity; this undoubtedly has implications for the supreme position that Paul ascribes to the Son of God (1:10) alongside of the Father.[32]

Clear the way for us to come to you (3:11). This request looks back to metaphor in 2:18 concerning the military practice of cutting up a road so as to make it impassable for a pursuing army (see comments on 2:18). Paul's prayer, therefore, is that God the Father and Jesus will remove the obstacles that Satan has used to block the apostle's path back to the Thessalonian church.

How to Live in Order to Please God (4:1–12)

In the first half of the letter body (2:1–3:10) Paul has been concerned with defending his integrity and reestablishing the confidence of his readers. This renewed trust in the apostle (and thus also in the gospel he proclaims) is necessary not only to encourage the Thessalonian believers in the midst of their persecution but also to ensure that they will obey the moral instructions he will now give them in the second half of the letter body (4:1–5:22). The technical term for such ethical teaching is "paraenesis," from a Greek word meaning "exhortation, advice."[33] After opening the paraenetic section of 1 Thessalonians with a general appeal to increase in conduct that is pleasing to God (4:1–2), Paul addresses the specific issues of holiness in sexual conduct (4:3–8) and brotherly love within the church community (4:9–12).

▶ Sexual Conduct in the Greco-Roman World

The Greco-Roman world had a tolerant attitude toward sexual conduct, particularly sexual activity outside marriage. Marriages were not usually love matches, but family arrangements. Typically, men in their middle twenties were paired with young women barely in their teens whom they had never met. So it was expected that married men would have sexual relations with other women, such as prostitutes, female slaves, or mistresses. This explains why Demosthenes (384–322 B.C.) could state matter-of-factly: "Mistresses we keep for our pleasure, concubines for our day-to-day physical well-being, and wives to bear us legitimate children and to serve as trustworthy guardians over our households."A-3 That attitudes had not changed at all some three centuries later is evident from the words of the Stoic philosopher Cato (95–46 B.C.), who praised those men who satisfied their sexual desires with a prostitute rather than another man's wife.A-4

A tolerant view of adultery and other sexual practices can also be seen from a variety of other sources. For example, funerary inscriptions reveal that concubinage was common. Prostitution was a business like any other, and profit from prostitutes working at brothels was an important source of revenue for many respectable citizens. Innkeepers and owners of cookshops frequently kept slave girls for the sexual entertainment of their customers. Adulterous activity was, in fact, so widespread that the emperor Augustus (63 B.C.–A.D. 14) established a new code of laws having to do with adultery and marriage—the "Julian Laws"—in a failed attempt to reform sexual practices. Within such a social context, it is not surprising that the Jewish Christian leaders of the Jerusalem church felt the need to include in their letter to Gentile Christians a warning "to abstain from sexual immorality" (see Acts 15:20, 29; 21:25). Paul issues the same warning to the Christians in Thessalonica (1 Thess. 4:3).

How to live in order to please God (4:1). The verb *peripateō* literally means "to walk" but has the metaphorical sense of "living one's life." It is not only one of Paul's favorite words to describe the Christian life (it occurs 32 times in his letters), it is also one of his more strategic terms as it is used to introduce themes that the apostle considered to be fundamental.[34] This metaphorical use of "walking" to describe moral conduct has its roots in Paul's Jewish background (approximately 200 of the 1547 occurrences of the Hebrew verb "to walk" in the Old Testament are metaphorical).

The metaphor also occurs in nonbiblical Greek (but with much less frequency and normally with a different verb, *poreuomai*) and thus would have been readily understood by Paul's readers.[35]

It is God's will that you should be sanctified (4:3a). The noun *hagiasmos*, which can be translated as "sanctification" or "holiness," is a key word in 4:3–8, occurring in various forms some four times. Holiness is an important Old Testament concept, which conveys the notion of "separation"—the need for God's covenant people to "come out" and be "distinct" from the surrounding peoples.[36] Holiness, therefore, is the boundary marker that separates God's people from all other nations. It is significant that Paul takes this standard of holiness, which had previously been the exclusive calling of Israel, and applies it here to the predominantly Gentile church in Thessalonica.[37]

Learn to control his own body (4:4). The noun *skeuos*, which literally means "vessel" or "household utensil," is used metaphorically here. One common interpretation takes *skeuos* as a metaphorical reference to "woman" or "wife," so that Paul is exhorting his readers "to take a wife" (RSV). A more likely interpretation views the noun as referring to one's own "body," so that the apostle commands

▶
DIONYSUS

A Herm (statue) of Dionysus from the crypt of the Serapeion in Thessalonica.

each of his readers to "learn to control his own body" (NIV; NRSV; NEB; JB). It is also possible that *skeuos* refers more specifically to the male sex organ. The noun in secular Greek had such a euphemistic use. The strongly phallic character of the Cabirus and Dionysian cults, which were popular at Thessalonica, also supports this meaning.

Who gives you his Holy Spirit (4:8). Paul picks up the language of the Old Testament prophets about the gift of God's Spirit as a key blessing for the Jewish people in the eschatological age—language associated with the "new" or "everlasting" covenant—and applies it to the predominantly Gentile Christians in Thessalonica. This is evident in the apostle's description of God's giving his Holy Spirit "into you," an expression that echoes exactly the words of Ezekiel (see Ezek. 37:6, 14 [LXX]; see also 36:27).[38]

Taught by God (4:9). The unique expression "taught by God" (*theodidaktoi*) is further evidence that Paul is making use of the "new covenant" language of the prophets and applying it to the predominantly Gentile church of Thessalonica. The apostle here alludes to Isaiah's description of the messianic age as a time when God will live so intimately in and among his people through his Spirit that they will no longer have to

---

▶ **Dionysus and Sexual Symbolism**

A statue of Dionysus was discovered in the temple of Serapis in Thessalonica. According to some mythical traditions, Dionysus suffered dismemberment. The legendary reconstitution of the god may have been ritually enacted by worshipers in the temple and would have affirmed the god's powers of renewal and regeneration. The sexual symbols and erotic activity associated with Dionysiac worship offer a possible background for the exhortations in 4:3–8 in general and for the meaning of *skeuos* in 4:6 in particular.[A-5]

be taught by human intermediaries, but will be "taught by God" (*didaktous theou*, Isa. 54:13; see also John 6:45, where Jesus quotes this same verse to show that "all will be taught by God" in the messianic age). Paul likely also has in mind Jeremiah's portrait of the new covenant as a period when God's people will not need others to teach them the law but will know it intimately, for God will write it on their hearts (Jer. 31:33–34).

Work with your hands . . . so that you will not be dependent on anybody (4:11b–12). The problem of idleness—Christians who refused to work—was an ongoing issue in the Thessalonian church. Paul first addressed this problem during the founding of the church (note the past tense in 4:11: "just as we told you"). He brings up the problem of idleness again in 1 Thessalonians, both here in 4:11–12 and later in 5:14 ("Warn those who are idle"). The problem apparently got

worse, thereby requiring Paul to address this matter yet again at greater length in 2 Thessalonians 3:6–15.

About Those Who Fall Asleep (4:13–18)

The Thessalonian church was confused over the fate of their fellow Christians who had died before Jesus' second coming. Unfortunately, it is not clear why the Thessalonians were "ignorant" (4:13) about this subject or what specific concern they had.[39] Paul's emphatic claim that living believers "will *certainly not precede* those who have fallen asleep" (4:15b) and that "the dead in Christ will rise *first*" (4:16b) before living believers suggests that the Thessalonian church worried that deceased believers would either miss out or be at some kind of disadvantage at Christ's return compared to those believers who are still alive on that day. After introducing the problem (4:13), Paul presents two arguments in response (an appeal in 4:14 to the church's confession about Christ's resurrection; an appeal in 4:15–17 to the "Lord's own word") before ending the discussion with a concluding exhortation (4:18).

Those who fall asleep (4:13). The use of "sleep" or "rest" as a euphemism for "death" is common, not only in biblical texts but in antiquity as well.[40] One should not find in this term, therefore, any support for the notion of "soul sleep," that is, that the soul exists in a nonconscious state of "sleeping" in the time between death and resurrection.

Grieve like the rest of men, who have no hope (4:13). Some Greek philosophers maintained that the soul was immortal and continued to exist after death. Certain

▶ **Tomb Inscriptions and the Afterlife**

Archaeologists have discovered many tomb inscriptions in Thessalonica. They illustrate how little expectation for a life after death existed in the Greco-Roman world. Being together with one's spouse in the grave is the final expectation. Paul contrasts this hopelessness by claiming that believers will be reunited not only with each other but also with Christ.

The text of one tomb inscription from Thessalonica reads: "...for this woman had this surname, while she was still among the living. Because of her special disposition and good sense, her devoted husband created this tomb for her and also for himself, in order that later he would have a place to rest together with his dear wife, when he looks upon the end of life that has been spun out for him by the indissoluble threads of the Fates" (*CIG* 1973).[A-7]

mystery religions also attempted to assure their initiates of afterlife. Such ideas, however, were not well defined and appear not to have been held at a popular level. The much more common attitude toward death was the sense of complete hopelessness that is reflected in the concise statement of Theocritus: "Hopes are for the living; the dead have no hope."[41]

Jesus died and rose again (4:14). The phrase "Jesus died and rose again" may well be a pre-Pauline, creedal formula of the early church.[42] By appealing to confessional material of the early church concerning Christ's resurrection, Paul comforts the Thessalonian believers with an authoritative teaching that not merely he but they also, along with all other churches, believe.

The Lord's own word (4:15). It is not clear whether Paul is referring to (1) a saying of Jesus not preserved in the Gospels; (2) a paraphrasing of Jesus' apocalyptic teaching, such as is found in Mark 13 and Matthew 24; (3) a general summary of Jesus' teaching; or (4) a teaching revealed to Paul on the Damascus Road or elsewhere. The "Lord's own word" likely consists of the material in verses 16–17a, with verse 15 containing Paul's summary of this saying of Jesus. By appealing to the "Lord's own word," Paul further comforts the Thessalonian believers by showing that he is not merely giving his personal opinion but that his words are in agreement with the authoritative teaching of the Lord Jesus himself.

Will be caught up together with them in the clouds (4:17a). This verse contains the one explicit reference in the New Testament to the "rapture"—the sudden removal of believers from earth and their reunion with Jesus in the air at the Second Coming. The word "rapture" does not actually occur here but originates from the Latin translation in the Vulgate of the Greek verb *harpazō*. Elsewhere, this latter term refers to the violent action of being "taken by force" or "snatched away," usually to the benefit of the one being taken.[43]

To meet the Lord in the air (4:17b). The Greek word used here, *apantēsis*, which

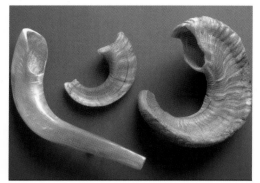

◀ *left*

SHOFAR

The ceremonial Jewish trumpet made of a ram's horn.

row, Irene writes: "But against such things [i.e., death], one can do nothing." She then ends her letter with words similar to that used by Paul in 4:18: "Therefore encourage each other." But whereas Irene appeals to the helplessness one has in the face of death, Paul holds before the Thessalonians the hope they have because of Jesus' resurrection (4:14) and Jesus' teaching (the "Lord's own word" in 4:15–17).

About Times and Dates (5:1–11)

Whereas 4:13–18 concerns the fate of *deceased* Christians at Jesus' return, 5:1–11 focuses on the fate of *living* Christians at the same eschatological event. The fact (1) that Paul two times reassures the believers in Thessalonica of what they already are ("sons of the light and sons of the day," 5:5; cf. v. 8), (2) that he reminds them that "God did not appoint us to suffer wrath" (5:9), and (3) that he exhorts them to "encourage one another and build each other up" (5:11), suggests that the Thessalonian Christians were not

lies behind the English translation "to meet," was a technical term in the ancient world. It referred to the meeting of a delegation of citizens from a city with an arriving dignitary in order to accord that visitor proper respect and honor by escorting him back to their city.[44] Such processions of leading citizens going out to welcome and accompany a visiting ruler or official back to the city were common in Hellenistic times.[45] The term *apantēsis* has this same sense in its two other New Testament occurrences: The wise virgins with their oil-filled lamps meet the bridegroom and escort him back to the banquet (Matt. 25:6); the Christians in Rome walk south to meet Paul on his prison journey and escort him back to the capital city (Acts 28:15). The picture that Paul presents, therefore, is of the church—consisting of both deceased (but now resurrected) and living Christians—meeting the descending Christ in the air and then escorting him back to earth.

Therefore encourage each other with these words (4:18). In a second-century A.D. letter (POxy 115) discovered in Egypt, a woman named Irene attempts to comfort grieving parents who have just suffered the loss of their son. After stating that she and her family have fulfilled the customary duties that express their sor-

REFLECTIONS

THE CONTRAST THAT PAUL MAKES IN 4:13 IS *NOT* that non-Christians grieve in the face of death whereas Christians do not express such sadness. Believers also grieve in the face of death. Such sorrow is natural, since death is not part of God's good created order but a painful consequence of the Fall. Death is not something that Christians happily embrace but an "enemy" (1 Cor. 15:26) that caused even the Lord Jesus to cry (John 11:35). Thus, tears in the face of death are not the sign of weak faith but of great love. But while Christians do grieve in the face of death just like non-Christians, there is an important difference: Christians grieve *with hope*. This hope is rooted in the knowledge that loved ones who have already passed away will in no way be at a disadvantage but will participate fully with living believers in glory of Christ's triumphal return.

merely curious about the timing of Christ's return but worried whether they were spiritually and morally worthy to meet the Lord on the day of his coming.[46]

About times and dates (5:1). Although the nouns translated as "times"(*chronōn*) and "dates" (*kairōn*) individually have distinguishable meanings, their tandem usage in the Septuagint (Dan. 2:21; 7:12; Wisd. Sol. 8:8) and the New Testament (Acts 1:7; 3:20–21) indicates that they together function as a conventional pair with a synonymous meaning. This stereotyped expression refers generally to the events of the end times and often is connected with the divine judgment that will take place then.

center ▶

"PEACE AND SAFETY"

A coin extolling the *Pax Augusti,* "the peace of Augustus."

The day of the Lord (5:2). In the Old Testament the expression "the day of the Lord" often refers to the time of divine judgment for the enemies of God (e.g., Obad. 15) and the time of deliverance for the people of God (e.g., Joel 2:31–32; Zech. 14:1–21). This double aspect of judgment and deliverance is also found in Paul's references to "the day of the Lord," which he also terms "the day of our Lord Jesus [Christ]" (1 Cor. 1:8; 2 Cor. 1:14), "the day of [Jesus] Christ" (Phil. 1:6, 10; 2:16), or simply "the Day" or "this day" (1 Cor. 3:13; 1 Thess. 5:4; 2 Thess. 1:10). Since this judgment and deliverance will take place at the return of Christ, the expression "the day of the Lord" is another way of referring to the "coming" (*parousia*) of Jesus (1 Thess. 4:15).

Like a thief in the night (5:2). The metaphor of a thief in the night likely originates in the teaching of Jesus (Matt. 24:43; Luke 12:39), which was later picked up by not only Paul but other New Testament writers as well (see 2 Peter 3:10; Rev. 3:3; 16:15). The apostle uses this metaphor to emphasize both the unexpectedness of the Day's arrival and its threatening character as a time of judgment for those unprepared.

While people are saying, "Peace and safety" (5:3). Although the phrase "peace and safety" may look back to Old Testament prophetic warnings against false claims of peace on the eve of national destruction, it more likely has in view the contemporary political environment, namely, Roman imperial sloganeering.[47] *Pax et securitas* ("peace and safety") was a popular slogan of the imperial Roman propaganda machine, and the concept of "Roman peace" was vigorously promoted through various media: coins (see picture above), monuments, and official proclamations. Rome held out to all those who submitted to its rule the promise of peace and safety, virtually an offer of "salvation" from unrest and danger.[48] Paul, however, has a stern warning for all those who trust in the political power of Rome instead of in God: "Destruction will come on them suddenly, as labor pains on a pregnant woman, and they will [certainly][49] not escape" (1 Thess. 5:3).

Darkness/light, night/day (5:4–8). The metaphors of darkness and light as well as night and day occur often in the Old Testament, Jewish literature (1QS 3:13–4:26; 1QM 1:1, 3), and Paul's other letters (Rom. 1:21; 2:19; 3:11–13; 1 Cor. 4:5; 2 Cor. 4:6; 6:14; Eph. 4:18; 5:8–11; 6:12; Col. 1:13).[50] "Darkness" and "night" symbolize alienation from God and ignorance about the imminent arrival of the day of the Lord; conversely, "light" and "day" symbolize closeness to God and an awareness about the coming day of judgment.

Sons of the light (5:5). The formulation "sons of the light" appears in Luke 16:8 but is best known for its frequent occurrence in the Dead Sea Scrolls, where it refers to the members of the Qumran community, who were anticipating their eschatological battle against the "sons of darkness," that is, all those who did not belong to their fellowship. Similarly, the designation "sons of light" serves to make a sharp distinction between the Thessalonian believers, who are prepared for the day of the Lord, and those outside the Christian community, who are unaware of the impending divine judgment they will receive at Christ's return.

Putting on faith and love as a breastplate, and the hope of salvation as a helmet (5:8). The imagery of armor originates in Isaiah 59:17, where God is said to "put on righteousness as a breastplate, and the helmet of salvation." Paul uses this military image both here and elsewhere in his letters to describe a variety of virtues with which Christians should arm themselves in the spiritual battle against Satan and his evil hosts.[51] The three virtues that the Thessalonians are exhorted to put on consist of the familiar triad of faith, love, and hope (see comments on 1:3).

For God did not appoint us to suffer wrath but to receive salvation (5:9). Paul comforts the Thessalonian believers by reminding them that their ultimate destiny on the day of the Lord rests not in their own work but in God's. This point was already made at the very beginning of the letter, when Paul states that God "has chosen you" (1:4), and it has been repeated a couple times thus far (2:12; 3:3). Here the apostle similarly claims that God has "appointed" or chosen these people of his not "to suffer wrath but to receive salvation."[52]

Final Exhortations (5:12–22)

At first glance, the exhortations in 5:12–22 appear to be something of a grab bag of diverse commands that have little connection with the Thessalonian church. A closer look, however, reveals a relatively clear structure through which Paul deals with four issues specifically connected to the situation in Thessalonica: esteeming congregational leaders (5:12–13); treating troubled congregational members (5:14–15); cultivating personal piety (5:16–18); and exercising spiritual gifts, especially prophecy (5:19–22).

▶ **"Peace and Safety" Provided by the Romans**

The Jewish historian, Josephus, records a decree from the citizens of Pergamum that praises the Romans for providing "peace [*asphaleia*] and safety [*eirēnē*]"—the same two words mentioned by Paul in 1 Thessalonians 5:3: "Decree of the people of Pergamum: 'In the presidency of Cratippus, on the first of the month Daisios, a decree of the magistrates. As the Romans in pursuance of the practices of their ancestors have accepted dangerous risks for the common safety [*asphaleia*] of all humankind and strive emulously to place their allies and friends in a state of happiness and lasting peace [*eirēnē*], the Jewish nation and their high priest Hyrcanus have sent as envoys to them....'"[A-8]

Those . . . who are over you in the Lord (5:12). The term *proïstamenoi* was used in secular Greek to refer to patrons or benefactors, that is, individuals who supported various clients or associations.[53] It may be, then, that Paul is referring here to wealthy individuals who, after being converted to Christianity, allowed their homes to be used as meeting places and provided financial and political support for the fledgling church. Such well-to-do people naturally became leaders, since the majority of the members belonged to the lower class and would not have the free time or education to work effectively in the congregation. One such patron of the Thessalonian church was Jason (Acts 17:5–9).

We urge you (5:14a). The verb *parakaleō* ("to urge, appeal") was part of an "appeal formula" commonly found in ancient letters to request that some action take place. This formula was used in official letters when kings and officials wanted to express a more friendly, less heavy-handed tone. Paul also uses the appeal formula in this nuanced manner, where his authority is not in question and he can make a request rather than a command in the confidence that his appeal will be obeyed.[54]

Warn those who are idle (5:14b). The first of three troubled groups in the Thessalonian congregation with whom Paul deals is "those who are idle" (*ataktoi*). This Greek word, used by the apostle four times in his two letters to describe this first group (the root *atakt-* occurs in 4:11; 2 Thess. 3:6, 7, 11), has two possible meanings.[55] One is derived from its use in military contexts to depict soldiers who would not keep step or follow commands—that is, those who were "obstinate" or "rebellious." The other stems from its use in the papyri of the Hellenistic period to describe students or workers who failed to do their work— that is, those who were "idle" or "lazy."[56]

▶

THESSALONICA
Archaeological remains of the Roman city.

The first meaning nicely captures the resistance of this group to their leaders (1 Thess. 5:12–14a), whereas the second meaning is supported by Paul's explicit commands to work found in both letters (4:11–12; 2 Thess. 3:6–15). It is best, therefore, to identify the first group here in 1 Thessalonians 5:14 as "rebellious idlers": members in the church who were not merely lazy but who obstinately refused to submit to the authority of their leaders and of the apostle. (For the cause of this group's problematic behavior, see "Why Did Some Thessalonian Christians Not Want to Work?" at 2 Thess. 3.)

Encourage the timid (5:14). The second troubled group addressed is the "timid" (*oligopsychoi*). This Greek word, which literally means having "little spirit/soul," occurs nowhere else in the New Testament and only rarely in other ancient writings so that it is difficult to deduce its precise meaning here. The usage of this word in the Septuagint signifies religious discouragement.[57] Paul, then, could be referring either to those who were shaken by the persecutions that the church had to endure (1 Thess. 2:14; 3:1–5) or to those who were anxious about various aspects of Christ's return (4:13–5:11).

Help the weak (5:14). The third troubled group with whom Paul deals is the "weak" (*asthenoi*). Although this Greek word can refer to physical weakness (i.e., those who are sick or ill), the larger context supports a reference to moral or spiritual weakness. Despite attempts to specify the weakness further (e.g., the refusal to eat certain foods [Rom. 14; 1 Cor. 8, 10], the struggle to live holy lives with respect to sexual conduct [1 Thess. 4:3–8], the anxiety surrounding "the times and dates" of the day of the Lord [5:1–11]),[58] there is not enough evidence to justify an exact identification.

Do not put out the Spirit's fire; do not treat prophecies with contempt. Test everything (5:19–22). The majority of the church's members—those who had "turned to God from idols" (1:9)—would have been all too familiar with various sorts of "ecstatic" activities practiced in the mystery religions and pagan cults. Some may have been leery of what appeared to be similar activities in the church and so attempted to limit the use of spiritual gifts such as prophecy.[59] But while Paul here affirms the work of the Spirit in general and prophecy in particular, he also seeks to regulate charismatic activity, calling on the Thessalonian believers to "test" everything that claims to be of the Spirit and "hold on to" only that which is found to be "good."

REFLECTIONS

THE DEEP MISTRUST AND DISDAIN in our modern culture toward authoritative structures has negatively impacted attitudes in the church toward those in leadership positions. Having rightly rejected a naïve trust in their pastor or other church leaders, many congregations have swung to the opposite extreme, treating those in a leadership position with a suspicion that borders on contempt. The church today, therefore, needs to both hear and heed Paul's exhortation to "respect" its leaders and "hold them in the highest regard in love because of their work" (5:12–13a).

Letter Closing (5:23–28)

Letters in the ancient world typically ended in brief fashion. Writers sometimes closed with final greetings, a health wish ("Take care of yourself in order that you may be well"), an autograph (some closing remarks written in the hand of the author rather than the secretary often employed to write the letter), a farewell wish (the Greek *errōso* literally means "Farewell" but has the colloquial sense of "Good-bye"), and the date. A first-century B.C. letter dealing with the matter of unirrigated land and the payment of taxes upon it, for example, ends: "Greet all your people. Athenarous and the rest of the children greet you. Take care of yourself in order that you may be well. Goodbye. Year 8, Epeiph" (POxy 1061).[60] Yet, the instances in which all—or even most—of these closing conventions occur simultaneously are rare.[61]

Although Paul's letter closings show that he was influenced by the epistolary practices of his day, they also reveal that the apostle was not limited to such practices. Paul cleverly adapts and expands the rather hackneyed epistolary conventions commonly found at the end of a letter such that his letter closings are truly unparalleled among extant letters of his day. In fact, the apostle carefully constructs his letter closings in such a skillful way that they relate directly to—sometimes, in fact, even summarize—the major concerns taken up in the bodies of their respective letters.[62]

May God himself (5:23–24). Instead of the simple and relatively fixed formula "May the God of peace be with you" (see Rom. 15:33; 2 Cor. 13:11; Phil. 4:9b), Paul in these verses has greatly expanded the peace benediction so that it echoes three major concerns addressed earlier in the letter: (1) The prayer for God to "sanctify you through and through" and for the Thessalonians to be "kept blameless" recalls the concern about proper conduct. (2) The reference to the "coming of our Lord Jesus Christ" echoes the concern about Christ's return. (3) The reassurance that "the one who calls you is faithful and he will do it" recalls the language of election and calling found in the letter (1 Thess. 1:4; 2:12; 4:7; 5:9)—language that comforts the Thessalonians in the midst of the persecution they are currently enduring.[63]

Greet all the brothers with a holy kiss (5:26). The practice of greeting others with a kiss, either when arriving or departing, occurs frequently in the Old Testament and the New Testament and so reflects a widespread custom in the ancient world.[64] The greeting kiss expressed not merely friendship but, more specifically, reconciliation and unity.[65] Paul's command to "greet all the brothers with a holy kiss," therefore, serves as a challenge to the Thessalonians to remove any hostility that may exist among them and to exhibit outwardly through the kiss greeting the unity they share as fellow members of the body of Christ.[66]

ANNOTATED BIBLIOGRAPHY

Best, Ernest. *A Commentary on the First and Second Epistles to the Thessalonians.* HNTC. New York: Harper & Row, 1972; reprint, Peabody, Mass.: Hendrickson, 1987.

A thorough treatment that still ranks as one of the best commentaries on the Thessalonian letters.

Gaventa, Beverly R. *First and Second Thessalonians.* Interpretation: A Bible Commentary for Teaching and Preaching. Louisville: John Knox, 1998.

A brief treatment that excels in its suggestions for application and preaching.

Holmes, Michael W. *1 & 2 Thessalonians.* NIVAC. Grand Rapids: Zondervan, 1998.

A judicious and readable exposition that applies the text in helpful and specific ways to contemporary culture and life.

Marshall, I. Howard. *1 and 2 Thessalonians.* NCBC. London: Marshall, Morgan & Scott, 1983.

A brief yet insightful commentary with an especially good and detailed discussion of introductory matters.

Wanamaker, Charles A. *Commentary on 1 & 2 Thessalonians.* NIGTC. Grand Rapids: Eerdmans, 1990.

An excellent full-length commentary on the Greek text that emphasizes rhetorical features of the letters.

Weima, Jeffrey A. D., and Stanley E. Porter. *An Annotated Bibliography of 1 & 2 Thessalonians.* NTTS 26. Leiden: Brill, 1998.

A helpful research tool that lists some 1200 works (the majority of which are annotated) that are germane for the interpretation of 1 and 2 Thessalonians.

CHAPTER NOTES

Main Text Notes

1. R. Riesner, *Paul's Early Period: Chronology, Mission Strategy, Theology* (Grand Rapids: Eerdmans, 1998), 341.
2. Cited by J. B. Lightfoot, *Biblical Essays* (London: Macmillan, 1893), 255.
3. See C. Edson, "Cults of Thessalonica (Macedonia III)," *HTR* 41 (1948): 153–204; K. P. Donfried, "The Cults of Thessalonica and the Thessalonian Correspondence," *NTS* 31 (1985): 336–56.
4. R. Jewett, *The Thessalonian Correspondence: Pauline Rhetoric and Millenarian Piety* (Philadelphia: Fortress, 1986), 126–32.
5. R. F. Hock, "The Workshop as a Social Setting for Paul's Missionary Preaching," *CBQ* 41 (1979): 438–50; A. J. Malherbe, *Paul and the Thessalonians* (Philadelphia: Fortress, 1987), 7–20.
6. 1 Thess. 2:2b, 14–15; 3:1–5; 2 Thess. 1:4–7; cf. Acts 17:5–7, 13; 2 Cor. 8:1–2.
7. J. L. White, *Light from Ancient Letters* (Philadelphia: Fortress, 1986), 39; P.CairZen I 59076.
8. For fuller treatments of the Pauline thanksgiving, see P. Schubert, *Form and Function of the Pauline Thanksgivings* (Berlin: Töpelman, 1939); P. T. O'Brien, *Introductory Thanksgivings in the Letters of Paul* (Leiden: Brill, 1977).
9. Rom. 15:18–19; 2 Cor. 12:12; see also Acts 14:3; 15:12.
10. See, e.g., Isocrates, *Demai* 4.11; Seneca, *Ep. Mor.* 6.5–6; 7.6–9; 11.9; Quintilian, *Inst. Orat.* 2.28; Philostratus, *Vit. Ap.* 1.19; 2 Macc. 6:2–28; 4 Macc. 9:23. A good introduction to these texts is A. J. Malherbe, *Moral Exhortation: A Greco-Roman Sourcebook* (Philadelphia: Westminster, 1986).
11. 1 Thess. 2:2, 14–15; 3:1–5; 2 Thess. 1:4–7; cf. Acts 17:5–7; 2 Cor. 8:1–2.
12. J. Barclay, "Conflict in Thessalonica," *CBQ* 55 (1993): 512–30.
13. So Donfried, "Cults of Thessalonica," 336–56; Jewett, *Thessalonian Correspondence,* 126–32.
14. For a fuller exploration of the historical issues lying behind Paul's defense in 2:1–16, see J. A. D. Weima, "An Apology for the Apologetic

Function of 1 Thessalonians 2.1–12," *JSNT* 68 (1997): 73–99.

15. BAGD, 203. See also L. Morris, *The First and Second Epistles to the Thessalonians* (Grand Rapids: Eerdmans, 1991), 62.

16. On the typical conduct of traveling orators, see B. Winter, "The Entries and Ethics of Orators and Paul (1 Thessalonians 2:1–12)," *TnyBul* 44 (1993): 55–74, esp. 60–64.

17. So, e.g., G. Fee, "On Text and Commentary on 1 and 2 Thessalonians," ed. E. H. Lovering Jr, *SBL 1992 Seminar Papers* (Atlanta: Scholars, 1992), 174–79; S. Fowl, "A Metaphor in Distress: A Reading of *NEPIOI* in 1 Thessalonians 2.7," *NTS* 36 (1990): 469–73; B. R. Gaventa, "Apostles as Babes and Nurses in 1 Thessalonians 2:7," in *Faith and History: Essays in Honor of Paul W. Meyer*, ed. J. T. Carroll (Atlanta: Scholars, 1991), 194–98.

18. Gaventa, "Apostles as Babes and Nurses," 193–207.

19. W. Michaelis, "σκηνοποίος," *TDNT*, 7:393–94; P. W. Barnett, "Tentmaking," *DPL*, 925–27.

20. For a broader discussion of issues surrounding Paul's manual labor, see R. F. Hock, *The Social Context of Paul's Ministry: Tentmaking and Apostleship* (Philadelphia: Fortress, 1980); *Pirqe ʾAbot* 2:2; 4:7.

21. See also 1 Cor. 4:14–15; Phil. 2:22; Philem. 10.

22. So, e.g., B. A. Pearson, "1 Thessalonians 2.13–16: A Deutero-Pauline Interpolation," *HTR* 64 (1971): 79–94; D. Schmidt, "1 Thess. 2:13–16: Linguistic Evidence for an Interpolation," *JBL* 102 (1983): 269–79.

23. F. D. Gilliard, "The Problem of the Antisemitic Comma Between 1 Thessalonians 2.14 and 15," *NTS* 35 (1989): 481–502.

24. See C. J. Schlueter, *Filling up the Measure: Polemical Hyperbole in 1 Thessalonians 2.14–16* (Sheffield: JSOT, 1994).

25. Josephus, *Ant.* 20.102–22.

26. This sentence bristles with grammatical and interpretive difficulties that cannot be treated here because of space constraints. The reader is directed to the commentaries for a fuller discussion.

27. G. Stählin, "ἐγκοπή, ἐγκόπτω," *TDNT*, 3:855–56.

28. On crowns in the ancient world, see W. E. Raffety, "Crown," *ISBE*, 1:831–32.

29. G. H. Whitaker, "Love Springs No Leak," *Expositor* 8th ser. 21 (1921): 126ff.; W. Kasch, *TDNT*, 7:585–87.

30. The punctuation adopted by the NIV results in three prayers, whereas the original Greek has only two.

31. So, e.g., Morris, *Thessalonians*, 107–8.

32. I. H. Marshall, *1 and 2 Thessalonians* (Grand Rapids: Eerdmans, 1983), 100.

33. See further M. B. Thompson, "Teaching/Paraenesis," *DPL*, 922–23.

34. J. O. Hollow, *Peripateô as a Thematic Marker for Pauline Ethics* (San Francisco: Mellen, 1992).

35. H. Seesemann, "πατέω," *TDNT*, 5:940–45.

36. N. H. Snaith, *The Distinctive Ideas of the Old Testament* (New York: Schocken, 1944), 24–32; see Ex. 19:5–6; Lev. 20:23–26; Deut. 26:18–19.

37. On this key point, see further J. A. D. Weima, "'How You Must Walk to Please God': Holiness and Discipleship in 1 Thessalonians," in *Patterns of Discipleship in the New Testament*, ed. R. N. Longenecker (Grand Rapids: Eerdmans, 1996), 98–119.

38. Weima, "How You Must Walk," 110–12.

39. For an overview of the five major hypotheses, see Marshall, *Thessalonians*, 120–22; for a sixth, see C. A. Wanamaker, *Commentary on 1 & 2 Thessalonians* (Grand Rapids: Eerdmans, 1990), 166.

40. Gen. 47:30; Deut. 31:16; 1 Kings 2:10; Job 14:12–13; Ps. 13:3; Jer. 51:39–40; 2 Macc. 12:45; John 11:11–13; Acts 13:36; 1 Cor. 11:30; Homer, *Iliad* 11.241; Sophocles, *Electra* 509.

41. Theocritus, *Idyll* 4.42.

42. The primary reasons are threefold: (1) the phrase "we believe" is used elsewhere to introduce a creedal formula (see Rom. 10:9); (2) Paul employs the name "Jesus" alone instead of his expected practice of referring to "Christ"; (3) the verb "rose" (*anestē*) is a rare one in Paul's writings as he normally employs a different verb to describe the resurrection of Christ (he uses *egeirō* thirty-seven times, whereas *anistēmi* occurs only twice).

43. Acts 8:39; 23:10; 2 Cor. 12:2, 4; Rev. 12:5.

44. E. Peterson, "ἀπαντήσις," *TDNT*, 1:380–81. This widely held understanding of the word *apantēsis* has been challenged by M. Cosby, "Hellenistic Formal Reception and Paul's Use of *APANTESIS* in 1 Thessalonians 4:17," *BBR* 4 (1994): 15–34. For a rebuttal to Cosby, see R. H. Gundry, "A Brief Note on 'Hellenistic Formal Receptions' and Paul's Use of *APANTESIS* in 1 Thessalonians 4:17," *BBR* 6 (1996): 39–41.

45. BGU 2.362.7.17; Polybius, *History* 5.26.8; Josephus, *Ant.* 11.8.4; Cicero, *Atticus* 8.16.2; 16.11.6; Chrysostom, *Thessalonians: Homily* 8.62.44.

46. M. W. Holmes, *1 & 2 Thessalonians* (Grand Rapids: Zondervan, 1988), 165. So also Marshall, *Thessalonians*, 132.

47. In addition to the brief remarks of Donfried, "Cults of Thessalonica," 344, see especially, H. L. Hendrix, "Archaeology and Eschatology," in *The Future of Early Christianity: Essays in Honor of Helmut Koester*, ed. B. A. Pearson (Minneapolis: Fortress, 1991), 107–18; Jer. 6:14; 8:11; Ezek. 13:10–16; Mic. 3:5.

48. Holmes, *Thessalonians*, 167.

49. The NIV fails to translate the emphatic negation found in the original Greek.

50. E.g., Job 22:9–11; Ps. 27:1; 74:20; 82:5; 112:4; Prov. 4:18–19; Isa. 2:5; 9:2; 60:19–20; 1QS 1:9–10; 3:13, 24–25; 1QM 1:1, 3.

51. Rom. 13:12; 2 Cor. 6:7; Eph. 6:11–18.

52. On the important and complex concepts of "wrath" and "salvation" in Paul's letters, see G. Borchert, "Wrath, Destruction," *DPL*, 991–93, and L. Morris, "Salvation," *DPL*, 858–62.

53. LSJ, 1526.

54. In addition to here, see 1 Thess. 4:1, 10b; also Rom. 12:1–12; 15:30–32; 16:17; 1 Cor. 1:10; 4:16; 16:15–16.

55. See G. Delling, "ἄτακτος, ἀτακτέω," *TDNT*, 8:47–48; C. Spicq, "ἄτακτος, ἀτακτέω, ἀτάκτως," *TLNT*, 1:223–26.

56. G. Milligan, *St. Paul's Epistles to the Thessalonians* (London: Macmillan, 1908), 152–54 ("Note G. On *atakteô* and its cognates").

57. Ex. 6:9; Isa. 35:4; Sir. 7:10.

58. So, respectively, E. Best, *The First and Second Epistles to the Thessalonians* (London: Black, 1972), 231; G. Fee, *God's Empowering Presence* (Peabody, Mass.: Hendrickson, 1994), 57, n. 75; D. A. Black, "The Weak in Thessalonica: A Study in Pauline Lexicography," *JETS* 25 (1982): 307–21.

59. So, e.g., Best, *Thessalonians*, 239; Holmes, *Thessalonians*, 183–84. Donfried ("Cults of Thessalonica," 342) writes: "One should not overlook the obvious parallels between the following texts and the mystery cults . . . 1 Thess. 5.19–22 where Paul explicitly urges his hearers not 'to quench' the Spirit but 'to test' it. Quite clearly the Apostle does not wish the gift of the Spirit to be confused with the excesses of Dionysiac mysteries; for Paul the Spirit does not lead to 'Bacchic frenzies'

but to joy precisely in the context of suffering."

60. White, *Light from Ancient Letters*, 107.

61. See J. A. D. Weima, *Neglected Endings: The Significance of the Pauline Letter Closings* (Sheffield: JSOT Press, 1994), 28–56.

62. Ibid., passim; see also J. A. D. Weima, "The Pauline Letter Closings: Analysis and Hermeneutical Significance," *BBR* 5 (1995): 177–98.

63. See the fuller discussion in Weima, *Neglected Endings*, 176–84.

64. For a listing of the relevant texts as well as a more detailed discussion of the kiss greeting, see G. Stählin, "φιλέω," *TDNT*, 9:119–46; S. Benko, "The Kiss," in *Pagan Rome and the Early Christians* (Bloomington, Ind.: Indiana Univ. Press, 1984), 79–102; W. Klassen, "The Sacred Kiss in the New Testament," *NTS* 39 (1993): 122–35.

65. See Gen. 33:4; 45:15; 2 Kings 14:33 (LXX); Luke 15:20.

66. See the fuller discussion in Weima, *Neglected Endings*, 111–14, 184–86; see also Rom. 16:16a; 1 Cor. 16:20b; 2 Cor. 13:12a.

Sidebar and Chart Notes

A-1. See further G. H. R. Horsley, "The Politarchs," *The Book of Acts in Its Graeco-Roman Setting*, eds. D. W. J. Gill and C. Gempf (Grand Rapids: Eerdmans, 1994), 419–31.

A-2. For an account of the suffering endured by Christians around the globe in the twentieth century, see James and Marti Hefley, *By Their Blood: Christian Martyrs of the Twentieth Century* (Grand Rapids: Baker, 1996); P. Marshall, *Their Blood Cries Out: The Untold Story of Persecution Against Christians in the Modern World* (Dallas: Word, 1997).

A-3. Demosthenes, *Orations* 59.122.

A-4. See also Horace, *Satire* 1.2.31–35.

A-5. Donfried, "Cults of Thessalonica," 337.

A-6. C. Colson, *The Body: Being Light in Darkness* (Dallas: Word, 1992), 46.

A-7. *Corpus Inscriptionum Graecarum*, ed. A. Boeckius (Hildescheim & New York: Georg Olms Verlag, 1977), 56.

A-8. Josephus, *Ant.* 14.10.22; trans. R. Marcus (LCL; Cambridge, Mass.: Harvard Univ. Press, 1933), 7.581.

2 THESSALONIANS

by Jeffrey A. D. Weima

Introduction

For comments on the city of Thessalonica and Paul's relationship with the church in that city, see the introduction to 1 Thessalonians.

Letter Opening and Thanksgiving (1:1–12)

Paul's letters always begin with the following fixed pattern: a listing of the sender(s), the recipients, a greeting, and then an extended thanksgiving to God for the faith and conduct of his readers. Although each of these features is typical of letters of that day, the apostle adapts and expands these conventions in a distinctly Christian way (see comments on 1 Thess. 1:1; 1:2–10).

Paul, Silas and Timothy (1:1). The inclusion of Silas and Timothy as cosenders, along with the frequent use of the plural "we" throughout the letter, might suggest that all three individuals mentioned in the letter opening functioned as the author of 2 Thessalonians. The use

CORINTH

Paul writes to the Thessalonians from Corinth.

▶ **2 Thessalonians**
IMPORTANT FACTS:

■ **AUTHOR:** Paul (despite his mentioning Silas and Timothy as cosenders).

■ **DATE:** A.D. 51 (Paul writes from Corinth).

■ **PURPOSES:**
- To commend the church for enduring persecution.
- To correct false teaching about the "day of the Lord."
- To discipline those living in idleness.

of the first person "I" in the letter closing (3:17; see also 2:5), however, as well as evidence from his other letters (see comments on 1 Thess. 1:1), indicates that Paul is the real author of this letter. The name of the second person is actually "Silvanus," whom the writer of Acts calls "Silas."[1] "Silvanus" is Silas's Latin name, which he would have as a Roman citizen (16:37).

We ought always to thank God for you (1:3). The obligation of human beings to give thanks to God is a common theme in both Jewish and Christian writings of this time.[2] The Mishnah, for example, in the context of reminding Jews during the Passover of how the Lord redeemed them from Egypt, states: "Therefore, we are obligated to thank him who wrought all these wonders for our fathers and us."[3] The Christian letter known as *1 Clement* exhorts its readers: "We ought in every respect to give thanks to him" (38:4). Similarly, the *Epistle of Barnabas* states: "The good Lord revealed everything to us beforehand, in order that we might know him to whom we ought to give thanks and praise for everything" (7:1; see also 5:3). Thus, the phrase "we ought always to thank God" (so also 2:13) does not mean that Paul views thanksgiving as a duty rather than a joy. Instead, the apostle is simply acknowledging, as do others of his day, the need for gratitude to be given to God, since he is responsible for the increased faith and love evident in the lives of the Thessalonian Christians.

All the persecutions and trials you are enduring (1:4). The suffering endured by the Thessalonian Christians started from the moment of their conversion (1 Thess. 1:6; 2:2; cf. Acts 17:5–7), continued during Paul's absence and the later visit of Timothy (1 Thess. 3:1–5), and had not ceased when 2 Thessalonians was written (2 Thess. 1:4–7). The kind of "persecutions" and "trials" that these believers experienced did not likely involve physical death or martyrdom,[4] since there is no evidence that the deaths in the church (1 Thess. 4:13–18) were a direct result of their faith. Instead, their suffering most likely consisted of social harassment—an experience that became all-too-common for Christians in the Greco-Roman world.

All this is evidence that God's judgment is right (1:5). The antecedent of "all this" is ambiguous[5] so that it is not clear what exactly Paul regards as "evidence" of God's just judgment. The traditional view sees "evidence" as looking back to "your perseverance and faith," so that it is the Thessalonian church's endurance of

▶ **Social Harassment of Christians in the Greco-Roman World**

Many sources, both within and without the New Testament, portray the resentment and offense felt by non-Christians when converts to Christianity refused to participate in normal social and cultic activities.[A-1] The exclusivity of the Christians' religion—their seemingly arrogant refusal to participate in or consider valid the worship of any god but their own—deeply wounded public sensibilities and even led to the charge that they were "atheists." Christians became easy targets of blame for earthquakes, floods, and agricultural failures, since these and other natural disasters were viewed as punishments from the gods, who felt slighted by this exclusive sect's failure to participate in cultic worship. Family members also felt a strong sense of betrayal over relatives who, on the basis of their newfound faith, broke ancestral traditions and showed an appalling lack of concern for their familial responsibilities.

oppression that shows God's just judgment.[6] A number of difficulties with this interpretation, however, has led to an alternative position: "Evidence" refers to the immediately preceding phrase ("persecutions and trials"), so that it is the sufferings of the church per se that constitute a sign of divine justice.[7] This interpretation is in keeping with a theology of suffering that can be found in Jewish literature of this period.[8] In these writings suffering is not viewed as a sign of God's rejection but somewhat paradoxically as a sign of God's acceptance insofar as he offers through it an opportunity for his elect to receive in this age the punishment for their few sins, thereby preserving the full measure of their reward in the age to come. At the same time suffering is also a sign of the absolute justice of God insofar as he insists on the punishment even of his elect.

God is just: He will pay back (1:6–7a).

The principle of divine retribution, the *lex talionis* ("an eye for an eye, a tooth for a tooth"), is frequently associated in the Old Testament with the day of the Lord. Isaiah 66:6, for example, states: "Hear that uproar from the city, hear that noise from the temple! It is the sound of the LORD repaying his enemies all they deserve." That this principle also lies behind 1:6–7a is evident in the play on words that God will pay back "*trouble* to those who *trouble* you and give *relief* to you who are *troubled*." The *lex talionis* is rejected as a principle of human conduct (Matt. 5:38–48; Rom. 12:17), since one may easily act unjustly or out of vindictiveness. These dangers do not exist in divine conduct, however, since "God is just," and so this principle forms an essential aspect of any teaching about God's judgment.[9] It also provides an answer to the problem caused

by the prosperity of the wicked and the suffering of the righteous, by looking to the future judgment to redress the injustice of this present life.[10]

This will happen when the Lord Jesus is revealed from heaven (1:7b).

The linking of the future return of Christ with the present suffering endured by the Thessalonian Christians suggests that Paul may have had in mind the concept of the "messianic woes." This was a widely held belief in the first century that the coming of the Messiah and/or the messianic age would be preceded by a period of intense suffering by God's people.[11] The notion of "messianic woes" may also explain the problem taken up in the next chapter. For if the Thessalonian believers viewed their suffering as part of the woes God's people would experience immediately prior to the return of Christ, they may have been more willing to believe the claim that "the day of the Lord has already come" (2:2).[12]

We constantly pray for you (1:11).

Letter writers in the ancient world often included at the beginning (and sometimes also the end) a reference to the fact that they were praying for the physical health and well-being of their recipients. In a letter that can be dated precisely to 168 B.C. a woman writes to her absent husband: "Isias to Hephaistion: Greeting. If you are well and your other affairs turn out in a like fashion, it would be as I have been continually praying to the gods"(PLond 1:42).[13] Two centuries later a man named Sabinianus similarly begins a letter to his brother Apollinarius by greeting him and stating: "I myself make daily prayers regarding your welfare before the local gods that you may be preserved for a long time" (PMich 8:499).[14] Paul also opens his letter to the Thessalonian church by letting these Christians know that he constantly prays for them. The prayers of the apostle, however, are not directed to Dionysius, Serapis, Isis, Cabirus, and the other gods worshiped in Thessalonica but to "our God," who is identified in the letter opening as "our Father and the Lord Jesus Christ." The content of Paul's prayers does not deal with his recipients' physical health but with their spiritual well-being, namely, that they may be "worthy of his [God's] calling" and that "the name of our Lord Jesus may be glorified in you" (1:11–12).

The Day of the Lord (2:1–17)

Paul had taught the Thessalonian believers about "the day of the Lord"—the events surrounding the return of Christ—already at some length during his original ministry in their city (see comments on 2:5). Thus, when he wrote in his first letter about the unexpected arrival of this day and the judgment that would take place then (5:1–11), the apostle could legitimately state that he did not really need to write about such things, since the Thessalonian Christians were already sufficiently well-informed about this future event, so that it would not surprise them like a thief in the night. Sometime after receiving this letter, however, the church was confronted with the claim that the day of the Lord had already come—a claim that caused them a great deal of consternation.

Paul responds by first urging the church not to be alarmed by this false report (2 Thess. 2:1–2). He then explains why it is impossible for the day of the Lord to have already arrived: There must first occur certain clearly defined events, foremost of which involves the appear-ance of the "man of lawlessness," who for the present time is being restrained (2:3–12). The apostle concludes his discussion with a thanksgiving (2:13–14), an exhortation (2:15), and a prayer (2:16), all of which are intended to comfort those shaken by the false report and to challenge the church instead to stand firm to the true teaching that he passed on to them.

Although the overview given above may sound relatively clear and simple, this passage has frustrated interpreters for centuries. For not only does Paul here make great use of apocalyptic imagery whose precise meaning is difficult to ascertain, the text also contains several grammatical irregularities and incompleted sentences. It is no exaggeration to claim that 2:1–17 is "probably the most obscure and difficult passage in the whole of the Pauline correspondence."[15]

Our being gathered to him (2:1). The immediate reference is to the comforting picture given in the previous letter of how all believers, both those who have already died and those who are still alive, will be gathered together to Jesus at his return (1 Thess. 4:16–17). This motif, however, goes back to the Old Testament hope in the gathering together of the scattered exiles to their own land on the day of the Lord and was taken over by Jesus and the early church to refer to the final gathering together of God's people with the Messiah.[16]

By some prophecy, report or letter (2:2a). Paul does not know for certain the means by which the false claim concerning the day of the Lord has been communicated. Thus, he lists three possibilities: a prophecy (the word used here literally is "spirit," but the NIV rightly sees this as a reference to a prophetic utterance), a report (lit., a "word," i.e., a nonecstatic spoken message), or a letter (either 1 Thessalonians or a forged letter attributed to the apostle). That Paul suspects a prophecy to be the most likely source is supported by two factors. First, Paul already anticipated in his first letter the need for the church to be more perceptive about "Spirit" utterances (1 Thess. 5:19–22). Second, this would explain why at the end of this passage the apostle exhorts the congregation to hold fast to what they have been previously taught by him "whether by word of mouth or by letter" (2 Thess. 2:15), but strikingly omits the first member of the triad in 2:2a "by some prophecy"—what Paul himself most likely believed to be the ultimate source of the false claim.[17]

The day of the Lord has already come (2:2b). The verb *enestēken* refers not to the imminence of the day of the Lord (KJV: "is at hand")[18] but rather to its actual presence (NIV: "has already come").[19] The Thessalonians did not likely view this day as a twenty-four period but as a complex period involving a number of events of which the return of Christ was just one part. They may have also viewed their own suffering as part of the "messianic woes," a period of severe distress before the appearance of the Messiah (see comments on 1:7b), and so been more willing to believe the claim that "the day of the Lord has already come."[20]

The man of lawlessness (2:3b–4). The man of lawlessness is typically identified with the Antichrist as well as the unnamed figure or figures who are expected to arise against Jesus prior to the time of his return.[21] The description of this figure here in 2 Thessalonians 2:3b–4 has striking similarities with a number

of Old Testament texts and events from the intertestamental period. For example, a number of the prophets describe pagan kings who made themselves out to be gods.[22] Or again, there are similarities with historical violations of the temple, such as when the Roman general Pompey in 63 B.C. entered the Most Holy Place and when the Roman emperor Caligula in A.D. 40 tried to set up a statue of himself there and so assert his claim to divinity.[23] The most probable situation, however, is that Paul is drawing from traditional material of early Christian eschatology that was based on the teachings of Jesus, who in turn incorporated the prophecy of Daniel in expounding his own views of the end times.[24]

I used to tell you these things (2:5). The imperfect tense of the verb (*elegon*) stresses the customary or repeated nature of the action: Paul had spoken often during his stay in Thessalonica about the man of lawlessness and his ultimate destruction at Christ's return.

What is holding him back / the one who now holds it back (2:6, 8). Paul states two times that the man of lawlessness and the rebellion associated with his appearance are currently being "held back"

THE JERUSALEM TEMPLE

A model of the temple and its courts.

or "restrained." The apostle first refers to the *thing* (neuter) that is restraining (2:6) and then later describes the *one* (masculine) who is restraining (2:8). This complicates even further the already difficult task of identifying the "restrainer" (see "Who Is the Restrainer?").

The Lord Jesus will overthrow with the breath of his mouth (2:8). Paul describes the destruction of the man of lawlessness with imagery borrowed from Isaiah 11:4 (LXX), where the Prince from David's house "will strike the earth with the word of his mouth and with the breath of his lips he will destroy the wicked." Other biblical and intertestamental passages employ identical or similar idioms dealing with the force of the mouth or breath to consume the unrighteous.[25]

But we ought always to thank God for you (2:13). See comments on 2 Thessalonians 1:3.

From the beginning God chose you (2:13). There are compelling reasons to replace "from the beginning" with the alternate reading found in the NIV footnote "as his firstfruits" (so also NRSV, NAB).[26] The word "firstfruits" (*aparchē*) refers to the part of the harvest that was the earliest to ripen and that consequently reassured the farmer of the fuller share of the harvest yet to come. Paul, therefore, reassures the small, persecuted, and alarmed church of Thessalonica that God has chosen them as "firstfruits"—the first of many more who will surely join them in "shar[ing] in the glory of our Lord Jesus Christ" (2:14).

Prayer for Paul and the Thessalonians (3:1–5)

Paul begins to bring his second letter to a close (note "Finally" in 3:1) by first issuing some general exhortations about prayer (3:1–5) before going on to specific commands about the "idlers" (3:6–15). The apostle starts with a request for prayer for himself and his coworkers (3:1–2) but then shifts the focus to the Thessalonian Christians (3:3–4) and his prayer for them (3:5).

▶ Who Is the Restrainer?

A wide range of suggestions has been made concerning the identity of the "restrainer"—the thing and person that Paul refers to in both impersonal and personal terms (2:6, 8):[A-2]

1. The Roman Empire and the Emperor
2. The Principle of Law and Order and the Political Leaders
3. The Proclamation of the Gospel and the Proclaimer (Paul or other missionaries)
4. The Power of God and God Himself
5. The Presence of the Church and the Holy Spirit
6. The Force of Evil and Satan
7. The False Prophecy and the False Prophet
8. The Jewish State and James of Jerusalem

There is a wide consensus that the restraining influence is positive and beneficial, which eliminates proposals 6 and 7. None of the remaining options, however, is free from difficulties either. Many scholars, therefore, are driven to the conclusion reached long ago by Augustine, who said of this passage: "I frankly confess that the meaning of this completely escapes me."[A-3]

We have confidence in the Lord (3:4). Ancient letter writers, after requesting something of the recipient, sometimes express confidence in the recipient's willingness or ability to grant the request. The author of PMich 485, for example, states: "I am confident, however, that you will show no hesitation at all in the matter mentioned above." Another ancient letter concludes: "Although I am absent, yet I am confident that my affairs will be greatly promoted by Your Mightiness—in this confidence I have written to you" (SB 7656).[27] Such statements of confidence served to exert indirect pressure on the recipient to grant the request and so live up to the confidence that the writer has in him.[28] Paul also includes in his letters similar statements of confidence, although he "Christianizes" them by claiming that his confidence in his readers is ultimately rooted "in the Lord," who is here said to be "faithful" and to "strengthen and protect you from the evil one."[29] Yet there still remains indirect pressure on the Thessalonian Christians to live up to the confidence that the apostle has in them.

Disciplining Idlers (3:6–15)

The problem of some believers living in idleness was a longstanding one in the Thessalonian church. Paul first addressed this issue during his initial visit to Thessalonica, when he commanded his converts to work.[30] He dealt once again with the problem of idleness, albeit briefly, in his first letter (1 Thess. 4:11–12; 5:14a). But instead of getting better, the problem apparently got worse. Thus, for yet a third time and at much greater length, Paul addresses in 2 Thessalonians 3:6–15 the issue of living in idleness. He begins and ends his extended treatment of the matter with commands to avoid those who are idle (3:6, 14–15) and sandwiches between these commands appeals both to the example that he and his coworkers set (3:7–9) and to his explicit teachings about work (3:10–13).

Keep away from every brother who is idle. . . . Do not associate with him (3:6, 14). Paul commands the larger church community to discipline those who are idle through the practice of social

---

▶ **Why Did Some Thessalonian Christians Not Want to Work?**

Eschatological reason. The traditional explanation involves the Thessalonians' eschatological excitement over the imminent return of Christ. The belief that Jesus would return soon caused some believers to abandon ordinary earthly pursuits, such as working for a living, so that they could give full attention to spiritual preparation, eschatological discussion, and perhaps preaching. This group likely reasoned to themselves: "Since the end is near, work is a waste of time."[A-4]

Sociological reason. The challenging explanation looks for a sociological cause. A few appeal to the general disdain toward physical labor prevalent in the Greco-Roman world.[A-5] More, however, turn to the patron-client relationship that was popular in that day.[A-6] In this relationship, members of the lower class attached themselves to benefactors from among the upper class, from whom they then received sustenance and help in various matters in exchange for the obligation to reciprocate with expressions of gratitude and support. It is argued that Paul's converts included those of the urban poor who had formed client relationships with wealthy members in the Thessalonian church, but who exploited the generosity of their new Christian patrons.[A-7]

ostracism.[31] The verb "keep away from" (*stellesthai*) in 3:6 is a rather general term of withdrawal or avoidance, and so it is not clear to what degree the errant members are to be shunned. The verb "associate with" (*synanamignysthai*) is more specific and suggests that discipline minimally involved exclusion from the formal activities of the church, such as corporate worship and the meal that was typically a part of the Lord's Supper celebration (1 Cor. 5:11; 11:17–34).[32]

Idle (3:6, 7, 11). There is some debate whether the Greek root *atakt-* refers to the problem of "idleness" or "rebelliousness" (see comments on 1 Thess. 5:14).

How you ought to follow our example / to make ourselves a model for you to follow (3:7, 9). The notion of imitating some sort of moral exemplar was common in the ancient world, especially by teachers who exhorted their students to imitate them.[33] Paul also makes frequent use of this concept in his letters as he holds up not only himself as examples to be emulated. In 2 Thessalonians 3:7–9, the apostle reminds the Thessalonian church that he and his coworkers worked long ("night and day") and hard ("laboring and toiling") in order to not to become a financial burden to anyone, even though as leaders they were entitled to monetary support ("not because we do not have the right to such help").[34] Such conduct serves as a powerful model for the Thessalonian believers—both those who are idle and those who are still working—on the importance of self-sufficient labor.

We worked night and day (3:8). On the kind of labor done by Paul and his companions, see comments on 1 Thessalonians 2:9.

"If a man will not work, he shall not eat" (3:10). Although Paul's maxim here has no exact parallel, similar sayings can be found in Jewish and early Christian literature. Rabbi Abbahu, for example, is cited as stating: "If I do not work, I do not eat."[35] The Greek text makes clear that Paul is not speaking about the inability to work but rather the *refusal* to work (the text literally reads: "If someone does not *want* to work. . ."). While the church must continue to care for those who genuinely need help (3:13, "never tire of doing what is right"),[36] it must not tolerate those who are unwilling to work. The *Didache*, an early Christian manual of instruction, makes the same point in its teaching on how to deal with visitors "who come in the name of the Lord": "If the one who comes is merely passing through, assist him as much as you can. But he must not stay with you for more than two or, if necessary, three days. However, if he wishes to settle among you and is a craftsman, let him work for his living. But if he is not a craftsman, decide according to your own judgment how he shall live among you as a Christian, yet without being idle. But if he does

REFLECTIONS

SOME TODAY ARE UNWILLING TO WORK, CONTENT rather to exploit the support provided by government welfare programs. Others, who are willing to work, view their labor only as a means to an end—that is, as the price they pay in order to obtain the pleasures of material wealth or weekend revelry (recall the popular acronym: T.G.I.F.—"Thank goodness it's Friday!"). The Scriptures teach, however, that work is a good creation gift instituted by God prior to the Fall (Gen. 2:15). Furthermore, Jesus is Lord over all areas of life—including the job site. Believers, therefore, ought to view their labor as one important way in which they serve Christ.

not wish to cooperate in this way [i.e., to work], then he is trading on Christ. Beware of such people."[37]

They are not busy; they are busybodies (3:11). The NIV nicely captures the wordplay in Greek at work here. Instead of being busy with their work (*ergazomenous*), the idlers are busybodies (*periergazomenous*), who spend their free time becoming a nuisance, presumably by meddling into the affairs of others and causing unrest. This is the same problem that likely lies behind Paul's command in his first letter "to lead a quiet life, to mind your own business and to work with your hands."[38]

Yet do not regard him as an enemy, but warn him as a brother (3:15). The emperor Marcus Aurelius observes that if someone behaves rudely in the gymnasia, it is best simply to "avoid him, yet not as an enemy," and that the proper approach generally to such people is "to avoid them but not look askance or conceive hatred for them."[39] In a somewhat similar way, Paul exhorts the majority of the Thessalonian church to "keep away from" (3:6) and "not associate with" (3:14) anyone who is idle but at the same time to treat such a person "not as an enemy" but "as a brother." The goal of discipline, therefore, is not punitive but redemptive. Although exclusion from the community will cause idlers initially to "feel ashamed" (3:14), they will hopefully respond with repentance and restoration to full fellowship within the community.

Letter Closing (3:16–18)

Second Thessalonians has a relatively brief letter closing. Yet it contains three of the four epistolary conventions typi-

cally found in the Pauline letter closings: a peace benediction (3:16), greeting (3:17), and grace benediction (3:18).[40] On the closing conventions typically found in ancient letters and Paul's skillful adaptation and expansion of these conventions, see introduction to 1 Thessalonians 5:23–28.

I, Paul, write this greeting in my own hand (3:17). It was common in the ancient world to have the help of a secretary (the technical term is an *amanuensis*) in the writing of a letter.[41] These letters typically end with an "autograph"—some final remarks written by the sender in his or her own hand. Since the change of script would have been obvious to the reader of the letter, there was no reason to state explicitly that the author was now writing rather than the secretary. Yet a few such statements can be found. The sender of PGren 89, for example, states: "I wrote all in my own hand," and the letters of Cicero similarly contain a number of references to *mea manu* ("in my own hand").[42] Paul also closes five of his letters with the phrase "in my own hand," thereby indicating that he is now taking over from the secretary to write personally to his readers.[43] Since the apostle knew that his letters would be read in a public gathering, where it would not be possible to observe the obvious change in handwriting style, he needed to state explicitly that the closing material was written in his own hand. The function of the autograph here in 2 Thessalonians 3:17 is not to emphasize the authenticity of the letter (as many scholars assert) but its authority, especially for those "idlers" whom Paul anticipates will not obey the exhortations this letter contains (see 3:14a).[44]

CHAPTER NOTES

Main Text Notes

For full bibliography of some works, see notes in 1 Thessalonians.

1. See 1 Thess. 1:1; 2 Cor. 1:19; 1 Peter 5:12; Acts 15:22–40; 16:19–29; 17:4–15; 18:5.
2. R. D. Aus, "The Liturgical Background of the Necessity and Propriety of Giving Thanks According to 2 Thess. 1:3," *JBL* 92 (1973): 432–38. Reprinted in R. D. Aus, *Barabbas and Esther and Other Studies in the Judaic Illumination of Earliest Christianity* (Atlanta: Scholars, 1992), 193–200.
3. *m. Pesaḥ.* 10:5.
4. Contrast Donfried, "Cults of Thessalonica," 349–50, and a few others.
5. This phrase is not in the Greek text but is implied by the construction.
6. So, e.g., Best, *Thessalonians*, 254–56; Bruce, *Thessalonians*, 149; Marshall, *Thessalonians*, 172–73.
7. Although this interpretation has been advocated for some time already in several German and French commentaries, it has only more recently appeared in English-language works: see J. M. Bassler, "The Enigmatic Sign: 2 Thessalonians 1:5," *CBQ* 46 (1984): 496–510; Wanamaker, *Thessalonians*, 220–23; B. Gaventa, *First and Second Thessalonians* (Louisville: John Knox, 1998), 102–3.
8. 2 Macc. 6:12–16; *2 Bar.* 13:3–10; 48:48–50; 52:5–7; 78:5; *Pss. Sol.* 13:9–10.
9. Rom. 2:6–8; 12:19; 2 Cor. 5:10; Col. 3:25.
10. See further Best, *Thessalonians*, 256–57; Marshall, *Thessalonians*, 174–75.
11. E.g., 1QH 3:2–18; Mark 13; Rev. 8, 9, 11.
12. So R. D. Aus, "The Relevance of Isaiah 66.7 to Revelation 12 and 2 Thessalonians 1," *ZNW* 67 (1976): 252–68, esp. 263–64; Wanamaker, *Thessalonians*, 224.
13. White, *Light from Ancient Letters*, 65.
14. Ibid, 183.
15. W. Neil, *The Epistles of Paul to the Thessalonians* (London: Hodder and Stoughton, 1950), 155.
16. Isa. 43:4–7; 52:12; 56:8; Jer. 31:8; Joel 3:1–2; Zech 2:6; 2 Macc. 2:7; Matt. 23:37; Mark 13:27; Luke 13:34.
17. Fee, *God's Empowering Presence*, 71–75. A fuller exposition of Fee's position is found in his "Pneuma and Eschatology in 2 Thessalonians 2.1–2—A Proposal About 'Testing the Prophets' and the Purpose of 2 Thessalonians," in *Telling the Mysteries: Essays in New Testament Eschatology in Honor of Robert H. Gundry*, eds. T. E. Schmidt and M. Silva (Sheffield: JSOT Press, 1994), 196–215.
18. So A. M. G. Stephenson, "On the Meaning of *enestēken hē hēmera tou kyriou* in 2 Thessalonians 2, 2," in *StudEvan IV*, ed. F. L. Cross (Berlin: Akademie Verlag, 1968): 442–51; Bruce, *Thessalonians*, 165.

ANNOTATED BIBLIOGRAPHY

Best, Ernest. *A Commentary on the First and Second Epistles to the Thessalonians.* HNTC. New York: Harper & Row, 1972; reprint, Peabody, Mass.: Hendrickson, 1987.

A thorough treatment that still ranks as one of the best commentaries on the Thessalonian letters.

Gaventa, Beverly R. *First and Second Thessalonians.* Interpretation: A Bible Commentary for Teaching and Preaching. Louisville: John Knox, 1998.

A brief treatment that excels in its suggestions for application and preaching.

Holmes, Michael W. *1 & 2 Thessalonians.* NIVAC. Grand Rapids: Zondervan, 1998.

A judicious and readable exposition that applies the text in helpful and specific ways to contemporary culture and life.

Marshall, I. Howard. *1 and 2 Thessalonians.* NCBC. London: Marshall, Morgan & Scott, 1983.

A brief yet insightful commentary with an especially good and detailed discussion of introductory matters.

Wanamaker, Charles A. *Commentary on 1 & 2 Thessalonians.* NIGTC. Grand Rapids: Eerdmans, 1990.

An excellent full-length commentary on the Greek text that emphasizes rhetorical features of the letters.

Weima, Jeffrey A. D., and Stanley E. Porter. *An Annotated Bibliography of 1 & 2 Thessalonians.* NTTS 26. Leiden: Brill, 1998.

A helpful research tool that lists some 1200 works (the majority of which are annotated) that are germane for the interpretation of 1 and 2 Thessalonians.

19. So the vast majority of commentators; see, e.g., Best, *Thessalonians*, 279; E. J. Richard, *First and Second Thessalonians* (Collegeville, Minn.: Liturgical, 1995), 325.

20. Aus, "Relevance," 263–64; Wanamaker, *Thessalonians*, 240.

21. 1 John 2:18, 22; 4:3; 2 John 7; Matt. 24:5, 23–24; Mark 13:21–22; Luke 21:8; Rev. 13.

22. Isa. 14:13–14; Ezek. 28:2; Dan. 6:7.

23. *Pss. Sol.* 2; 17:11–14; Josephus, *Ant.* 14.4.4; Philo, *Embassy* 203–346; Josephus, *Ant.* 18.8.2–9.

24. Matt. 24; Mark 13; Dan. 7:25; 8:11; 9:26–27; 11:31, 36.

25. Ps. 32:6; 134:17; *1 Enoch* 14:2; 84:1; Job 4:9; Isa. 30:27–28; Rev. 19:15; *1 Enoch* 62:2; *4 Ezra* 13:10–11; *Pss. Sol.* 17:24, 35.

26. The difference in Greek between the two readings is only the addition or omission of a single letter. For a fuller discussion of the textual issues involved in this reading, see Fee, "On Text and Commentary," 179–80; idem, *God's Empowering Presence*, 77, n. 142; Holmes, *Thessalonians*, 252, n. 4.

27. Both letters are cited in S. N. Olson, "Pauline Expressions of Confidence in His Addressees," *CBQ* 47 (1985): 282–95.

28. Olson ("Pauline Expressions," 289) states: "The evidence of a variety of parallels suggest that such expressions [of confidence] are usually included to serve the persuasive purpose. Whatever the emotion behind the expression, the function is to undergird the letter's requests or admonitions by creating a sense of obligation through praise."

29. Gal. 5:10; 2 Thess. 3:4; Philem. 24; 2 Thess. 3:3.

30. 1 Thess. 4:11b; 2 Thess. 3:6, 10.

31. See also 1 Cor. 5:2, 5, 13; 2 Cor. 2:5–11; cf. Matt. 18:15–18.

32. For a more extended discussion, see J. T. South, *Disciplinary Practices in Pauline Texts* (Lewiston, N.Y.: Mellen, 1992).

33. See the texts cited above in note 9.

34. In addition to 2 Thess. 3:7, 9, see 1 Cor. 7:7–16; Gal. 4:12–20; Phil. 1:30; 4:9a; 1 Thess. 1:6; but others: God (Eph. 5:1); Christ (1 Cor. 11:1; Phil. 2:5–11; 1 Thess. 1:6); the churches of Judea (1 Thess. 2:14); Timothy (Phil. 2:19–24); Epaphroditus (Phil. 2:25–30).

35. *Gen. Rab.* 2.2 on Gen. 1:2.

36. See also Gal. 6:10; Eph. 4:28; 1 Tim. 5:3–8; Titus 3:14; as well as Paul's collection for the needy believers in Judea (Rom. 15:26–29; 1 Cor. 16:1–4; 2 Cor. 8–9; Gal. 2:10).

37. M. W. Holmes, ed., *The Apostolic Fathers*, trans. J. B. Lightfoot and J. R. Harmer (Grand Rapids: Baker, 1992), 265–66; *Did.* 12:2–5.

38. 1 Thess. 4:11; see also 1 Tim. 5:13.

39. This potential parallel with 2 Thess. 2:14 was first proposed by J. Moffatt, "2 Thessalonians iii. 14, 15," *ExpTim* 21 (1909–10): 328; Aurelius, *Meditationes* 6.20.

40. The only item missing is a hortatory section—some final commands or exhortations. On the various closing conventions found in Paul's letter closings, see Weima, *Neglected Endings*, 77–155.

41. See E. R. Richards, *The Secretary in the Letters of Paul* (Tübingen: Mohr-Siebeck, 1991); Weima, *Neglected Endings*, 45–50.

42. E.g., *Ad. Att.* 8.1; 13.28. See also Richards, *Secretary*, 173.

43. These five references, along with the personal comment of the secretary himself in Rom. 16:22 ("I, Tertius, who wrote down this letter, greet you in the Lord"), strongly suggest that Paul used an amanuensis in the writing of all his letters, even those in which he does not explicitly state that he is now writing "in my own hand" (see Weima, *Neglected Endings*, 118–26); 1 Cor. 16:21; Gal. 6:11; Col. 4:18a; 2 Thess. 3:17; Philem. 19.

44. So Marshall, *Thessalonians*, 232; Weima, *Neglected Endings*, 126–27.

Sidebar and Chart Notes

A-1. I am heavily indebted for the following to Barclay, "Conflict in Thessalonica," 513–16.

A-2. For an explanation and evaluation of these proposals, see Marshall, *Thessalonians*, 196–99; Wanamaker, *Thessalonians*, 250–52; L. Morris, "Man of Lawlessness and Restraining Power," *DPL*, 592–94.

A-3. Augustine, *City of God*, 20.19.

A-4. So, e.g., Best, *Thessalonians*, 175, 230, 331; Morris, *Thessalonians*, 130, 253.

A-5. So, e.g., Marshall, *Thessalonians*, 116, 223.

A-6. So, e.g., R. Russell, "The Idle in 2 Thess. 3:6–12: An Eschatological or Social Problem?" *NTS* 34 (1988): 105–19; B. Winter, "'If a Man Does Not Wish to Work. . .': A Cultural and Historical Setting for 2 Thessalonians 3:6–16," *TynBul* 40 (1989): 303–15.

A-7. There does not appear to be enough evidence available to determine with any high degree of certainty whether the eschatological or sociological reason is correct. For a discussion of the strengths and weaknesses of each position, see Weima, "'How You Must Walk,'" 113–15.

1 TIMOTHY

by S. M. Baugh

The Pastoral Epistles

First and Second Timothy and Titus have been termed the "Pastoral Letters" since the eighteenth century. Many scholars today think that these letters were written by a later follower of Paul and not by the apostle himself. Their reasons center on vocabulary and style, but recent research into the role of secretaries in ancient compositions has provided convincing explanation for the stylistic differences between the Pastorals and the other Pauline letters.

The tedious mechanics of writing, even among the well educated, was usually left to a secretary or even to a close friend, while the author concentrated on communicating the substance of his thought.[1] This is only natural, since polished oratory was the main goal of ancient higher education and the epitome of civilized life; written works were only secondary forms of communication, which were even then often designed to be read aloud in public (cf. Rev. 1:3).[2] The first-century Jewish author Josephus explicitly mentions

EPHESUS

The countryside surrounding the ancient city.

▶ 1 Timothy
IMPORTANT FACTS:

- ■ **AUTHOR:** The apostle Paul.
- ■ **DATE:** About A.D. 65 (after Paul's first Roman imprisonment).
- ■ **VENUES:** Paul is probably in Macedonia writing to Timothy at Ephesus.
- ■ **OCCASION:**
  - • To warn and inform Timothy about false teachers in the Ephesian area.
  - • To establish certain guidelines for church practices.
  - • To encourage Timothy in the conduct of his ministry.

secretaries who assisted him in his major compositions; two of his later works "are so different that one would hardly suppose them to be contemporary productions from the same pen."[3]

Furthermore, we should actually expect differences of style and content in the Pastorals from Paul's other letters. Paul wrote to his close associates, Timothy and Titus, who were fully versed in his teaching and practice, whereas letters like Romans or Colossians were written to churches who often needed extensive instruction from the apostle in more fundamental areas (cf. 1 Cor. 3:1–3). The Pastoral Letters naturally fit the picture of a senior missionary pastor writing to his associates on the kind of pastoral issues they can expect to face in their church planting ministry.[4]

Therefore, we can safely accept the Pauline authorship of the Pastorals. Even if a secretary helped Paul compose his letters, "the author assumed complete responsibility for the content and exercised this duty usually by checking, editing, or even correcting the draft."[5]

**WESTERN ASIA
MINOR**

▼

The Occasion of First Timothy

All three Pastoral Letters present particular problems if we try to line them up with the chronology of Paul's life presented in Acts. While it appears to be possible to place the writing of 2 Timothy during Paul's custody in Caesarea (Acts 23–26), this creates more problems than it solves, since, for example, Demas had abandoned Paul in 2 Timothy 4:10, whereas he was with Paul after his transfer to Rome (Col. 4:14; Philem. 24). As a result, most scholars who accept Pauline authorship of the Pastorals understand a scenario like the one that follows.

The book of Acts ends with Paul in custody in Rome awaiting trial before Caesar. Paul had to wait over two years under house arrest in Rome for this trial to begin (Acts 28:30–31). The delay came because the Jewish authorities from Jerusalem had to appear personally at the trial in order to press charges and to make the case for the prosecution.

A law passed by the Roman senate in A.D. 61 discouraged anyone from making frivolous charges and from causing undue delay of legal process. The imperial authorities took stern measures against plaintiffs who did not appear in court to press their cases, so we must assume that there was pressure on the Sanhedrin in Jerusalem to send a delegation to Rome to prosecute Paul.[6] However, the mid-60s was a turbulent time in Jerusalem. The Jewish Sanhedrin was about to lose everything in the bloody insurrection of the Zealots, which broke out in A.D. 68 and ended in the decimation of Jerusalem and of its temple two years later—hence their delay in prosecuting Paul. It is conceivable that the problems in Jerusalem prevented the Jewish authorities from ever sending a prosecuting delegation to Rome. In such a case, the Romans may have released Paul, but with a stigma on his record.

After this first Roman imprisonment, Paul apparently spent more time ministering in Ephesus, where he left Timothy to carry on while he went to Macedonia (1 Tim. 1:3). Paul intended to return to Ephesus at some point (3:14; 4:13), but whether he did or not is unknown. First Timothy was probably written during the time Paul was in Macedonia.

During the same period after Paul's release from Rome, he had spent some time in Crete and left Titus there to carry on the work (Titus 1:5). Paul had made some inroads for the gospel while on his way to Rome (Acts 27), and it is reasonable to assume that he would return to further establish a church on this island and then leave behind a close associate like Titus to carry on the work. It was after this trip that Paul, while on his way to or already in Nicopolis in western Greece, wrote the letter to Titus.

Whether Paul actually arrived at Nicopolis is unknown; perhaps he had arrived and then returned to Asia Minor. It appears from hints in 2 Timothy (e.g., 2 Tim. 4:12–20) that Paul was arrested a second time in either Troas or elsewhere in Asia Minor and was again sent to Rome for trial. Perhaps the hostile Jewish elements in Asia Minor recorded in Acts instigated this second arrest. Second Timothy was apparently written during the time of this second Roman imprisonment. Paul now expects to be condemned to death (4:16–18). If his first Roman trial (i.e., where Acts ends) had concluded without a clear exoneration, the Roman authorities would have found a second arrest itself sufficient reason to condemn Paul.[7] He was a threat to public order, and as such they would have held him in chains "like a criminal" while awaiting trial (2:9). The Romans were obsessed with public order and were ready to punish any danger to the *pax Romana* with severe measures.

If this scenario is correct, the Pastoral Letters were Paul's final letters and fit into the end of his apostolic ministry. First Timothy would have been the first letter written, followed by Titus, then

◄

EPHESUS

At the beginnng of Curetes Street, two columns depict Hercules draped in a lion skin.

2 Timothy. Paul himself appears to be conscious of the impending end of his ministry, and he wants to securely ground the next generation in apostolic doctrine, practice, and pastoral insights, as well as to warn his associates of the threat of heresy and false teachers. This well accounts for the pastoral content of these letters and how they differ so much from Paul's more general letters to churches.

Timothy was prone to have been somewhat shy and abstemious in character (e.g., 1 Tim. 5:23). With Paul having just escaped Roman custody with his life, one can understand the uncertainties of ministry in the first century. As a result, Paul explains why he is writing 1 Timothy: "I am writing you these instructions so that, if I am delayed, you will know how people ought to conduct themselves in God's household" (1 Tim. 3:14–15). In other words, Timothy does not need a doctrinal handbook—he knew the gospel and the Scriptures well (2 Tim. 3:15)—

but he did need some practical advice on ecclesiastical matters and some encouragement to overcome his hesitancy because of his youth and relative inexperience (1 Tim. 4:12–16). That is precisely what Paul provides here. No one enjoys confrontation, and thus Paul also had to warn Timothy of the menace of heretical teaching in the church and how to confront it.

Salutation and Letter Opening (1:1–2)

Paul opens his letter to Timothy in much the same way as his other letters, yet with the distinctive focus on his apostolic appointment "by the command of God our Savior and of Christ Jesus our hope." Paul is not trying to magnify his ministry over against Timothy's but to assure his follower in the ministry that the "deposit" (2 Tim. 1:14) he is passing on to him is the genuine, divinely originated faith, not

---

▶ False Teachers in the Pastoral Letters

The precise tenets of the false teachers of whom Paul warns Timothy and Titus are difficult to determine. In part this is understandable, since they undoubtedly did not invite Paul to their meetings! They seem to be proto-Gnostic teachings (1 Tim. 6:20) colored by Jewish, pagan, and occult ideas and practices. And it is possible that Paul is warning against more than one group of false teachers, some of whom are from "the circumcision group" (Titus 1:10). Paul does provide us with a sketch of some of their main notions: devotion to myths, genealogies, and "godless chatter," a misguided and ill-informed focus on the law and "Jewish myths," ascetic practices, and teaching that the resurrection has already taken place.[A-1]

Paul further indicates that the false teachers

can also be spotted by a display of their evil motives, such as greed (1 Tim. 6:5; Titus 1:11). They can also be known by the evil things that accompanied and are produced by their teachings: controversies and factional strife (1 Tim. 1:4; 6:4–5), quarrels over words (6:4; 2 Tim. 2:14; Titus 3:9), and "foolish and stupid arguments" (2 Tim. 2:23), rather than "love, which comes from a pure heart and a good conscience and a sincere faith" (1 Tim. 1:5). The source of this gangrenous false teaching is ultimately the devil and his demons (4:1; 2 Tim. 2:26). Paul does give hope that this false teaching will not ultimately triumph against the truth of God: "But they will not get very far because, as in the case of those men, their folly will be clear to everyone" (2 Tim. 3:9).

the fabrications of the false teachers of whom he is about to warn him (see also Rom. 16:26; Titus 1:3).

Timothy my true son (1:2). Paul refers to Timothy as "my true son in the faith" (cf. 2 Tim. 2:1; Phil. 2:20, 22). The word "true" here can refer to a "natural" child. The first-century Alexandrian Jewish writer, Philo, for instance, uses this word to say that the Egyptian princess regarded Moses "as though her *natural* child."[8] The word can also refer to a "legitimate" versus an illegitimate child.[9] Here, Paul uses the term metaphorically: "my true son *in the faith*." An interesting papyrus document uses this adjective "true" when it records the adoption of a nephew by a man: "that he might be your *true* son and firstborn as though born to you from your own blood."[10] Paul says, in effect, that Timothy is his heir in ministry and his representative to the church in Ephesus.

False Teachers (1:3–7)

Into Macedonia (1:3). It is not certain that Paul was still in Macedonia when he wrote this letter, but it is a reasonable possibility (cf. Titus 3:12). Macedonia, the homeland of Alexander the Great, was (and still is) a region to the north of Greece extending northwest to Illyricum (Rom. 15:19), north to the Balkan area, and east to Thrace. The capital of the Roman province of Macedonia was Thessalonica, and Berea—where Paul's ministry was so nobly received (Acts 17:10–13)—was the seat of its provincial assembly. An important overland road called the *Via Egnatia* ("Egnatian Road") ran from Asia Minor through the Macedonian cities of Philippi and Thessalonica on its way to the Adriatic Sea. Paul had first gone to Macedonia

as a result of a vision (16:9–10) and had an eventful time in the region, to say the least (16:11–17:15; 20:1–2).

Stay there in Ephesus (1:3). In Paul's day, Ephesus was fast becoming, in the grandiose language found on many of its later public documents, "the chief and greatest Mother-City ("metropolis") of Asia" (e.g., *Inschriften von Ephesos* [hereafter = *IvE*] 24) and "the largest emporium in Asia this side of the Taurus."[11] Paul had spent a considerable time evangelizing and teaching in Ephesus (Acts 18:19–20:1), and it was to become a chief center for the spread of early Christianity. In the early second century, Ignatius commented on the large size of the church there ("your multitudinousness").[12] According to tradition, the apostle John and Mary, Jesus' mother, made their home in Ephesus as well. Ephesus forms an important backdrop to 1 and 2 Timothy, and because it has been the subject of thorough archaeological investigation for the past century, evidence

R E F L E C T I O N S

WHEN PAUL SAYS, "THE GOAL OF THIS COMMAND IS love," (1 Tim. 1:5) he is pointing to the instructions that Timothy is to command the opponents (cf. 2 Tim. 2:25–26). One can also more generally see that the outcome of all Christian instruction is love, which itself flows out of the great, spiritual benefits of the work of Christ: "a pure heart," which is a central requirement for seeing God (Matt. 5:8; cf. Ps. 24:4; 51:10; 2 Tim. 2:22); "a good conscience," which was brought into effect once and for all by the high priestly sacrifice of Christ (Heb. 9:14; 10:22; cf. 1 Tim. 1:19; 3:9; 4:2); and "a sincere faith," which is a faith "without hypocrisy" (contrast 1 Tim. 4:2). This lovely fruit of good teaching stands in stark contrast to the wrangling and division caused by the heretical teachers.

from this city will be brought in repeatedly throughout our commentary.

Paul sent Timothy to Ephesus in order to "command certain men not to teach false doctrines any longer" (1:3; cf. 6:3). This is not the last place in the Pastoral Letters where false teachers will be identified and warned against—it is a central theme of these letters.

Myths and endless genealogies (1:4). We are not quite sure what precise group engaged in such tiresome wrangling over "myths and endless genealogies." Was this a proto-Gnostic group? One feature of later Gnosticism was belief in a continuous emanation of being in discrete levels from a divine center like ripples on a pond. Some scholars think that these ranks of emanations could be called "genealogies." However, these might be "myths," but not "genealogies." Others point to the genealogies in the Old Testament and propose a Jewish group here. This seems more likely, given the syncretistic tendencies of the day. Paul possibly encountered a Jewish group who had amalgamated Hellenistic theosophical notions with biblical ideas.[13] Ignatius of Antioch, the early second-century Christian martyr and church leader, warned the church at Magnesia on Maeander (located about fifteen miles southeast of Ephesus) against "heterodoxies and ancient myths" connected with living "according to Judaism."[14]

"Myths and genealogies" were also a stock feature of the popular pagan literature of the day. The second-century B.C. historian Polybius contrasted his prosaic account of history with storytellers who dealt with "matters concerning genealogies and myths."[15] Earlier he had typified the target audience of this kind of literature: "The genealogical side appeals to those who are fond of a story, and the account of colonies, the foundation of cities, and their ties of kindred, such as we find, for instance, in Ephorus [ca. 405–330 B.C.], [it] attracts the curious and lovers of recondite lore."[16]

Teachers of the law (1:7). The opponents whom Timothy is to reprove want to be "teachers of the law." This is one word in Greek, *nomodidaskaloi* (lit., "law teachers"), and is only found elsewhere to refer to the Jewish scribes (Luke 5:17; accompanying the Pharisees) and a designation for Paul's teacher, Rabbi Gamaliel (Acts 5:34; cf. 22:3). Here the false teachers are concentrating on the law of Moses but do not understand the truth of the law despite their self-assurance. The Greek cities at the time revered certain "lawgivers" who were considered as founders of their civilization, much like the founding fathers of America. The most eminent was the sixth-century B.C. poet Solon, whose constitution and laws gave a distinctive direction to classical Athens.[17]

▶

CHRYSIPPUS, A FAMOUS TEACHER

He was the successor of Cleanthes as the head of the Stoics (280–207 B.C.).

The Law's Proper Use (1:8–11)

In its prohibitive function, the law does not address the law-abiding but lawbreakers. The list Paul gives of sample lawbreakers (1:9–10) seems generally comprehensible to us: rebels, murderers, and perjurers are punishable by modern laws. Yet our civil laws do not condemn all of the acts Paul lists here, like sin, adultery, or "perversion" (i.e., sodomy), nor did ancient civil laws; but they are a transgression of God's eternal covenant law (Isa. 24:5–6).

The ungodly and sinful, the unholy and irreligious (1:9). Ancient civil laws prohibited irreligion in various forms. One has only to read Acts 19:37 to see that blaspheming a state deity (in this case Artemis Ephesia) was a serious charge on a level with temple-robbing. Consider also that seditious impiety was one of the two capital charges successfully brought against Socrates by the Athenians, which led to his execution by suicide.[18]

Those who kill their fathers or mothers (1:9). Patricide and matricide are a singular horror for many peoples. In ancient Greek and Roman society, honor of one's parents was highly valued, so that, for example, even the unintentional murder of his father brought an indissoluble stain of guilt (Greek, *miasma*) on Oedipus, the subject of Greek tragic plays. Matricide was still a hot topic in Timothy's day, for in A.D. 59 the Emperor Nero had arranged for a shipwreck to get rid of his meddlesome mother, Agrippina—who was herself widely suspected of poisoning her husband, Emperor Claudius, to make room for Nero. The shipwreck plot failed, for Agrippina swam to safety, so Nero sent an assassin to do the job as she

was recovering from her narrow escape. In a (melodramatic) play written by an anonymous author after Nero's death, Agrippina appears as a vengeful ghost, saying in part: "Among the dead the memory still lives of my foul murder, the infamous offense for which my ghost still cries for vengeance."[19]

Slave traders (1:10). When Paul mentions "slave traders" among the list of gross lawbreakers, he is not mentioning an activity that was strictly illegal at the time—quite the contrary. Timothy could not have missed the prominent trade in slaves at Ephesus, which served as a wholesale market for slaves being sent from inland Asia Minor and other Eastern points of origin to the Roman West. Timothy would have seen the statue, possibly in the Ephesian marketplace, of C. Sallustius Crispus Passienus, Roman proconsul of Asia in A.D. 42/3, dedicated by "those who trade in the slave market" (*IvE* 3025). This and another similar Latin inscription from the time of the Emperor Trajan (*IvE* 646) indicate that the slave market was run by a Roman guild of slave traders. Hence, the slave trade itself was not illegal.

But how were these slaves acquired to begin with? The word for "slave trader" can also mean "kidnapper." The association of these two ideas is not coincidental, since there were five main sources for slaves in antiquity: captives in war, children of slaves, foundlings (children "exposed" [i.e., thrown out to die] by their parents and picked up by someone to be raised as their slaves), debt bondage, sale of oneself or one's children into slavery out of extreme poverty, and illegal kidnapping of free persons by brigands and pirates. The latter appear often in the literature of the period (e.g., the romantic novel by Xenophon of Ephesus, *Ephesiaca*). In real life, Paul often faced the threat of kidnapping during his missionary trips through inland Asia Minor (2 Cor. 11:26), especially during his trips through the narrow pass of the Taurus mountains (the "Cilician Gates") just west of Tarsus. This pass was a notorious place for ambush by bands of cutthroats.

The sound doctrine (1:10). Evil practices conflict with "sound doctrine." The word often rendered "sound" modifies "doctrine" or "words" in the Pastoral Letters. It comes from a word meaning "to be healthy" and contrasts with the gangrenous character of heresy. Christian doctrine brings spiritual health, and holiness of life is an integral outcome of Paul's gospel (1:11). Paul stresses that he was personally entrusted with this gospel in order to encourage his successor in the ministry by showing that the gospel he passes on to Timothy was of divine origin.[20]

Paul Was Shown Mercy (1:12–17)

Paul now focuses on the mercy of Christ Jesus on sinners, of whom Paul lists himself the premier example as a "blasphemer and a persecutor and a violent man" (1:13; cf. Acts 7:58–8:3; 9:1–2). In Paul's case, he was shown mercy not only because he acted in unbelief, but as a public demonstration of the tender mercies and grace of the Savior (1 Tim. 1:16).

A trustworthy saying (1:15). This "trustworthy saying" is the first of five occurrences of this kind of citation in the Pastoral Letters.[21] The saying here is brief and merely points to the purpose of Christ's incarnation: "to save sinners."[22]

To the King eternal (1:17). Paul closes this section with praise in a form I call an "ascription hymn" (though it may actually be a prayer, not a song). There are usually three elements to this format: specification of the recipient ("to the King eternal, immortal, invisible"), an "ascription" of certain blessed characteristics ("honor and glory"), and a closing with the solemn Jewish affirmation of the truth of the statement, "Amen." This type of format is also found, for instance, in the Book of Revelation in important places ascribing divine blessing both to God who sits on his heavenly throne and to the victorious Lamb.[23]

Instruction and Warning (1:18–20)

Fight the good fight (1:18). Comparing the Christian life with a contest or a fight is fairly common.[24] There is a parallel exhortation using the same key Greek words in *4 Maccabees*, an early first-century A.D. book. During a gruesome scene, one of seven Hebrew brothers under torture by King Antiochus IV ("Epiphanes"; reigned 175–64 B.C.) commends his brothers to follow his example of perseverance: "Fight the sacred and noble battle for religion" (*4 Macc.* 9:24).

Shipwrecked (1:19). Hymenaeus and Alexander, of whom only Hymenaeus is mentioned elsewhere (2 Tim. 2:17), and others are said to have "shipwrecked their faith." This image is powerful anywhere, but particularly at Ephesus, which was one of the most important seaports and shipping distribution points in the eastern Mediterranean. The shipwreck image was also vivid for Paul, of course, since "three times I was shipwrecked, I spent a night and a day in the open sea" (2 Cor.

11:25). With the small size of sailing craft in those days (see the box on 2 Tim. 4:21), lack of compass and other navigational aids, and the unpredictable storms at certain times of the year in the Mediterranean (late fall through early spring; cf. Acts 27:9), shipwrecks and drowning were all too common events for travelers by sea. Hence, shipwreck became a fairly common metaphor for tragedy or downfall in life: "A son born to the timocratic man at first emulates his father, and follows in his footsteps; and then sees him suddenly dashed, as a ship on a reef, against the state, and making complete wreckage of both his possessions and himself . . ." (Plato, *Republic* 553A–B; LCL trans.).

Instructions on Corporate Prayer (2:1–8)

First Timothy 2–3 concern the corporate life the church. This is a natural subject for Paul to address, given the late stage in his missionary career. He must have realized at this point that he had to make provision for the regular administration of the church after the apostolic period. The other Pastoral Letters demonstrate this same concern and account for some of the differences of style and content with Paul's other letters. The section before us begins and ends with an exhortation to regular prayer in the churches.

Prayers . . . for everyone (2:1). As Paul establishes church practice in this section and those that follow, it is notable that prayer forms the heart of the church's continuing ministry. By God's condescension and grace, he allows our "requests, prayers, intercession and thanksgiving" to have a role in his sovereign government of the world's affairs. A

typical interest of Paul as the apostle to the Gentiles (2:7; cf. Gal. 2:7–8) is that the church's prayers must be made for "everyone." In other words, prayer reaches out to all kinds of people. The word "everyone" in the NIV—*pantas anthrōpous* in Greek—can be better rendered "all kinds of people." In the plural, the Greek word for "all" (*pantes*) often refers inclusively to classes of people or of things—as it does later in this letter: "For the love of money is a root of *all kinds of* evil" (1 Tim. 6:10). There can be no discrimination whatsoever in our intercession and ministry.

For kings (2:2). Paul gives as examples of the sorts of people for whom we should pray "kings and all those in authority" (cf. Titus 3:1). There were only a few actual rulers with the title of "king" in Paul's day, though none in the territory surrounding Ephesus. The Romans had looked back to the expulsion of King Tarquinius Superbus some six centuries earlier by L. Junius Brutus as the founding of their republic. Hence, Roman emperors never dared take on the title "king," even when most sorely tempted—"Lord and god" perhaps (Suetonius, *Domitianus*, 13), but never "king." Yet the Greek-speaking people generically referred to high rulers, including the Roman emperors, as "kings," and the title

NERO

He was the reigning "king" of the empire when Paul wrote this letter (A.D. 54–68).

came to correspond roughly to "sovereign" in English.[25]

And all those in authority (2:2). The people "in authority" in Ephesus at the time were both the Roman provincial governor and the local city officials, the latter of which included the Secretary of the People (Acts 19:35), city councilors, the market director, and others with official or semi-official powers. Paul asks the church to pray for Nero and other pagan leaders, in order that they might guarantee a stable society in which the church could prosper and "live peaceful and quiet lives in all godliness and holiness."

This is good and pleases God (2:3). Paul's statement about God's will in the next few verses needs to be interpreted carefully in light of what precedes and follows. In particular, Paul grounds prayer for all kinds of people in God's approval and good pleasure (2:3). This is an important qualification: If we are to be assured that God hears and answers our prayers, we must pray for the kinds of things he approves. Otherwise, he will not necessarily grant our requests. But for prayers such as those in 2:1–2, we can pray with full assurance of God's ready acceptance

and favorable response. Why? Why is God ready to hear requests and intercessions even on behalf of the likes of Nero? Paul addresses that question directly in 2:4–7 in the profoundest manner, so we must trace out his argument carefully next.

Wants all men to be saved (2:4). The "all men" whom God desires to be saved points us to his people derived from all the families of the earth. This is clear when we take 2:5–7 into view. Paul's argument can be paraphrased like this: If God is one, and there is only one Mediator with one way of redemption, and if God has chosen me to save *some* of the Gentile peoples in the scope of my apostolic mission, then we can legitimately conclude that God desires *any sort of person to be saved* regardless of ethnic origin. This was true in Old Testament times only on rare occasions, but now it is the norm by which the worldwide missionary effort of Christianity must be guided.

For there is one God (2:5). Paul rather abruptly invokes the oneness of God as substantiation for his understanding of God's will to save all kinds of people—not just Jews. The affirmation that there is only one God came naturally to Jews,

REFLECTIONS

THE CONCLUSION WE MUST DRAW
from Paul's argument in 1 Timothy 2:1–8 is that any type of prejudice in the church's outreach, whether social, ethnic, racial, or otherwise, is inimical to the will of God. And we can and must pray for those still-unreached groups of peoples today with the same passion and assurance Paul had, whom God expressly desires us to reach with his gospel of grace and to call his people out "from every tribe and language and people and nation" (Rev. 5:9; cf. 7:9).

for whom the *shema* (Heb. "hear") of Deuteronomy 6:4 ("Hear, O Israel: The LORD our God, the LORD is one") acted as a banner and summary of their religion over against the polytheism of all of their neighbors (e.g., James 2:19). This same axiom is used by Paul elsewhere, as here, to establish that there is only one way of salvation for all people, not just the Jews, and that is the way of faith in the one Mediator, Jesus Christ.[26] (The argument of 1 Tim. 2:5, by the way, is far too subtle for a forger to reproduce and is one of the indelible marks of Paul's authorship of 1 Timothy.)

Who gave himself as a ransom (2:6). Christ is said to have offered himself as a "ransom" (or "redemption price") for all his people, not just those who are Jewish (cf. 1 John 2:2). It is the price paid to set us free (cf. Titus 2:14).[27]

The testimony given in its proper time (2:6). Testimony to what? To God's purpose to move redemption beyond the confines of Palestine in this age—some-

thing he had planned from the beginning (Gal. 3:8). Indeed, this is such a monumental point that Paul feels compelled to assure his friend that it is true in a most sober way: "I am telling the truth, I am not lying" (1 Tim. 2:7). One must read this passage in light of the worldwide unfolding of God's redemptive program. Now is the time. God has essentially issued a worldwide imperial edict: "In the past God overlooked such ignorance, *but now he commands all people everywhere to repent*" (Acts 17:30; emphasis added).

I was appointed a herald (2:7). Paul calls himself a "herald" of the true faith. Heralds were the most common medium of public communication in the days before newspapers. Timothy would have heard them often at Ephesus at funeral processions or any public meeting. A sacred

herald (*hierokeryx* or just *keryx*) was also linked with various cults, including that of Artemis Ephesia. He led the formal rites and publicly recited the prayers.[28]

Lift up holy hands (2:8). Here Paul assumes that the church will adopt the Old Testament posture of supplication and of worship. "Hear my cry for mercy as I call to you for help, *as I lift up my hands* toward your Most Holy Place"; "*Lift up your hands* in the sanctuary and praise the LORD."[29]

Instructions on Church Order (2:9–15)

Paul continues his directions for the public ministry of the church. Here he focuses on women in the church. The historical background of this section of Scripture has often been misinterpreted, so we must proceed carefully with an eye fixed on the actual historical sources.[30]

Women to dress modestly (2:9). It was customary for women in ancient Greek cities to dress up in their very finest for public worship festivals. For instance, the historian Herodotus remarks that the Athenian women gathered in a temple precinct at the summons of a tyrant "in their best clothes as if they were off to a festival" (5.93). The romance novel by Xenophon of Ephesus opens with a great procession in honor of the patron goddess of Ephesus, Artemis Ephesia, at which all the young girls march in process in their very finest clothes, "for it was the custom at this festival to find husbands for the girls and wives for the young men."[31] Even the cult statues of goddesses were adorned in great finery at public festivals. At Ephesus, the statue of Artemis was dressed by young girls who

held an official title of "Adorner" (*kosmeteira*; e.g., *IvE* 2, 892, 983–84, 989).

In contrast to the prevailing practice, Paul instructs women (and, by implication, men as well) to focus their attention not on rich wardrobes, but on the inner beauty of Christian character. This instruction is not new or novel (e.g., 1 Peter 3:3–4); as Ignatius of Antioch puts it: Christians are a new Temple for God, appointed to be "shrine-bearers, Christ-bearers, sanctity-bearers, dressed up from head to toe in the commandments of Jesus Christ."[32]

Not with braided hair (2:9). In Paul's day, hairstyles were undergoing a radical change. Earlier in the Greek world, women's hairstyles were simple: The hair was pinned in the back and held up with a simple band or scarf. In public, respectable women would wear veils on the top of the head, which fell down the back to the shoulders and hid any elaborate hairdo. Only a shady woman or one

in mourning would appear in public with her hair untied and unveiled.[33] However, in the mid-first century, women throughout the empire were copying the elaborate braided and ornamented hairdos of the Roman empresses (many of whom were quite scandalous).[34]

A woman should learn in quietness. . . . I do not permit a woman to teach (2:11–12). These two verses are drawing an ever-increasing amount of comment today, but Paul's injunctions in 1 Timothy 2:11–12 require no special historical insights to understand.[35] He says that women are not called to serve in the office of teacher or of elder in the church. A crucial distinction to understand here is that between special and general office ministries. Ordained men are called to a special office by Christ (e.g., Rom. 10:15; Eph. 4:11), while nonordained men and all women in the church have a general office to serve the Lord in various capacities. If we did not have the chapter division between 1 Timothy 2:15 and 3:1 (which is a modern invention), this special office context of Paul's statements on women in 2:11–12 would be more obvious to us, since he

1 Timothy

▶ Was Ephesus a Feminist Culture?

There are abundant indicators in the historical remains of ancient Ephesus that it cannot be characterized as a feminist culture. Although its state deity was a goddess, many other states whose patriarchal character has never been questioned also worshiped goddesses (e.g., classical Athens worshiped Athena). The nature of a culture as feminist must be demonstrated through what we can know about its *institutions*, particularly its political, religious, social, and cultural institutions. So, for example, were the political figures of ancient Ephesus women or men?

The answer to this question is clearly that they were men like: Tib. Claudius Balbillus who had an Ephesian festival named after him (*IvE* 3041–42; the "Balbilleia"); the General, Prytanis, and Secretary of the People (Acts 19:35); Heraclides son of Heraclides son of Heraclides (a noble line) (*IvE* 14, 1387); L. Cusinius Velina the Overseer of Ephesus (the same word found in 1 Tim. 3:1) and Secretary of the People under Gaius and Claudius (*IvE* 659B, 660B, et al.); or the famous Asiarch Tib. Claudius Aristio, whom Pliny the Younger calls "the chief man (*princeps*) of the Ephesians" and whose political enemies forced him to appeal to Caesar as had Paul a few decades earlier.[A-2] These aristocratic men not only steered the ship of state and were at the pinnacle of Ephesian society and culture, they also filled and managed all the chief religious priesthoods and boards that ran the magnificent banking, agricultural, and fishing enterprise that was the temple of Artemis of Ephesus.

Ephesian women were indeed priestesses of Artemis and of other goddesses, but this was the norm in the Greco-Roman world, not a sign of feminism—or equally inaccurate, a sign of sacred prostitution.[A-3] Let us illustrate this point with but one example here.[A-4] An elaborate public funeral was established for the noble M. Antonius Albus (*IvE* 614C) and his wife Laevia Paula (*IvE* 614B) at Ephesus a few decades before Paul lived there. The inscription commemorating this lavish affair records that the funeral procession was accompanied by a herald who announced the following to all the spectators: "The Council and Citizenry hereby crowns Laevia Paula, daughter of Lucius, who led a modest and decorous life." The Greek word rendered "modest" here is the adjective form of a word found in 1 Timothy 2:9, "with decency and *propriety.*" Paul's contemporaries at Ephesus would have agreed that "propriety" or "modesty" was a female virtue, not radical feminism.[A-5]

proceeds directly to the requirements for male overseers of the church in 3:1–7.

Let us be clear that Paul is *not* forbidding women in 2:11–12 from teaching men in private out of their general office as believers (e.g., Acts 18:24–28), from discipling their children (cf. 2 Tim. 1:5; 3:15) and younger women in the church (Titus 2:3–4), or from participating in and giving leadership in hospitality (1 Tim. 5:10) or in other kinds of ministries and service to the Lord (e.g., Acts 9:36; Rom. 16:1–2). However, Paul clearly says as apostolic instruction (1 Tim. 2:7) that a woman should "learn in quietness and full submission . . . she must be silent" when it comes to the official teaching and ruling ministry of the church.

It has been asserted that Ephesus was such a haven for ancient feminism that Paul is only speaking about *Ephesian* women being in submission to male church officers here. However, this is not what he says *prima facie*. Paul's statements in these verses were meant to be taken as parallel with those addressed to men "everywhere" (2:8). It can be demonstrated that Ephesian culture was not driven by any kind of underlying feminist or egalitarian ideology, even though individual women or groups in antiquity may have expressed views along these lines from time to time (see accompanying box).

For Adam was formed first (2:13–15). Paul roots his instructions on male-female relations in the church in 2:9–12 squarely in the creation order. This effectively shows that his instructions have direct cross-cultural application.[36] Adam was created first, and similar to the rights given to the firstborn son in the Old Testament, who often held special rights (e.g., Num. 3:2ff.; cf. *Bekhorot* 8), this gave Adam a certain official role and responsibility in the covenant family. Hence, it was *his* sin that brought death into the world, not Eve's (Rom. 5:12–21; 1 Cor. 15:21), even though Eve sinned first (1 Tim. 2:14; cf. Sir. 25:24), because Adam was the covenant head (cf. Hos. 6:7). And Adam's sin could only be reversed by Christ in his official role as "last Adam" (1 Cor. 15:45); indeed, Adam originally "was a pattern of the one to come" (Rom. 5:14). It is because of this structure that God has given the official role to teach and lead only to certain sons of Adam. Other believers hold what historically has been called the "general office of believer," with all of its own rights and responsibilities.[37]

Instructions on Church Office (3:1–13)

Overseer (3:1). The Greek term for "overseer" (*episkopos*) was used in secular Greek with a fairly broad range of meanings for someone who watched over someone else. This could be a tutor who watches over students, a soldier or a watchman who watches over a city, a guardian deity, or any kind of "guardian" (as 1 Peter 2:25). Paul uses *episkopos* here and in the parallel passage in Titus 1:6–9 as an alternative expression for an "elder" (*presbyteros*), which brings out the elder's role as a "guardian" of the welfare of the Christian churches under his care. This is clear from Paul's famous farewell speech to the elders of Ephesus, when he called these "elders" to meet him at Miletus (Acts 20:17) and said in part: "*Keep watch* over yourselves and all the flock of which the Holy Spirit has made you *overseers*. Be *shepherds* of the church of God, which he bought with his own blood"

(Acts 20:28; emphasis added). One can see from the highlighted words that an "overseer" was an elder in his role as a kind of guardian or watchman. As 1 Timothy 3:9 shows, the overseer was also to be a teacher of "deep truths of the faith."

The overseer must be above reproach (3:2). For the requirement of the elder to be the "husband of but one wife" (3:2; cf. 3:12; 5:9; Titus 1:6), see the comments on Titus 1:6. Paul insists on high moral standards for both the overseer (3:2–7) and the deacon (3:8–12) candidate. In the pagan world, such standards would only have a remote parallel with certain priesthoods in a city like Ephesus. For example, we read on extant Ephesian public inscriptions that certain priestesses served the state goddess, Artemis Ephesia, "with piety and decorum" (e.g., *IvE* 989A). And since Artemis was herself a virgin goddess (not a mother goddess, as some people think), it was required that her priests and priestesses themselves observe complete chastity while fulfilling their priestly term of office. This is evident on the following two examples, where "purely" refers to sexual purity (cf. Pausanias 8.13.1): "To Good Fortune. I, C. Scaptius Frontinus, *neopoios* [a temple overseer], City Counselor, along with my wife, Herennia Autronia, give thanks to you, Artemis, that I have completed a term as Essene *purely* and piously" (*IvE* 1578B; emphasis added); and, "The State Council and People honor Mindia Menandra, daughter of Gaius Mindius Amoenus, who completed her term as Priestess of the goddess *purely* and generously" (*IvE* 992A; emphasis added).

Beyond this, however, pagan priesthoods in the Greek world were often sold to the highest bidder and had no stringent moral requirements.[38] In Rome, the priesthoods were acquired through patronage connections (the Roman emperors held the highest priesthood with the title of *pontifex maximus* in the imperial period) and were usually held for life. As in the Greek world, priesthoods of Rome were usually reserved for the wealthy and well-born. Paul's statements about qualification for church office show a much different set of requirements. It is not wealth or nobility of birth that qualifies one to the Christian ministry, but a divine call (Rom. 10:14), as evidenced in part by a high moral character.

He must manage his own family well (3:4). Household management was the subject of a number of treatises in antiquity, including Xenophon's famous Socratic essay, the *Oeconomicus* (Greek for "household management"). In Xenophon's essay, the husband instructs his fourteen-year-old bride (the average age for marriage among Greek and Roman girls was fourteen to sixteen) on her vital role in managing the household resources, including the care and supervision of household slaves, while he

A MAN AND HIS FAMILY

A funerary stele from the Thessaloniki Museum.

▼

supervised the gathering of produce from the farms. Because of the presence of slaves and freedmen in an average ancient household, management of sometimes large households could be demanding. An inscription from Philadelphia regulating a household cult evidences a large ancient household and its management (see accompanying box).

Deacons, likewise . . . (3:8–10, 12–13). The qualifications for deacons are similar to those for overseers. Both are to be self-controlled, free from avarice, monogamous, good managers of their households, and so forth. The primary difference seems to be that the overseer must be "able to teach" (3:2), though both officers must have a firm grasp on Christian doctrine (3:9; cf. Titus 1:9). In both cases, the behavior of church office-holders must be above reproach for the sake of the church's health, the testimony of the church before the world, and their own consciences before the Lord.

In the same way, their wives . . . (3:11). Paul inserts the statement in 3:11 in the middle of his specification of deacon qualifications. The NIV translates: "In the same way, [their] wives are to be women worthy of respect. . ." (emphasis added; "their" is not in the Greek original). In the margin, however, the NIV translators pro-

---

▶ An Ancient Household Cult

We possess an inscription from Philadelphia in Lydia (Rev. 3:7–13) from the late second to early first century B.C., which regulated a household cult in a private household. Each household in antiquity typically had its own private cult in addition to members' participation in public or in other private cults. In this inscription, we find the head of the house managing the details of his household's behavior and cult practices. The text reads as follows (the word *oikos* is Greek for "household" or "house"):

> May Good Fortune Prevail. For health and common salvation and the finest reputation the ordinances given to Dionysius in his sleep were written up, giving access into his *oikos* to men and women, free people and slaves. . . . When coming into this *oikos* let men and women, free people and slaves, swear by all the gods neither to know nor make use wittingly of any deceit against a man or a woman, neither poison harmful to men nor harmful spells. They are not themselves to make use of a love potion, abortifacient, contraceptive, or any other thing fatal to children; nor are they to recommend it to,

nor connive at it with another. They are not to refrain in any respect from being well-intentioned towards this *oikos*. If anyone performs or plots any of these things, they are neither to put up with it nor keep silent, but expose it and defend themselves. Apart from his own wife, a man is not to have sexual relations with another married woman, whether free or slave, nor with a boy nor a virgin girl; nor shall he recommend it to another. . . . A free woman is to be chaste and shall not know the bed of, nor have sexual intercourse with, another man except her own husband. But if she does have such knowledge, such a woman is not chaste, but defiled and full of endemic pollution, and unworthy to reverence this god whose holy things these are that have been set up. She is not to be present at the sacrifices, nor to strike against (?) the purifications and cleansings (?), nor to see the mysteries being performed. But if she does any of these things from the time the ordinances have come on to this inscription, she shall have evil curses from the gods for disregarding these ordinances.[A-6]

vide an alternative: "deaconesses" for "their wives." The key word in the Greek text is *gynaikes* (where we get *gynecology*), which is the ordinary word for either "women" (e.g., 1 Tim. 5:2) or, in many contexts, "wives" (e.g., Eph. 5:22). The two renderings represent the two main interpretations of this verse.

The first view, represented in the NIV main text, takes the "women" here as "wives" of the deacons, since Paul's statement in 3:11 is imbedded in the midst of his discussion of male deacons' qualifications (e.g., *husband* of one wife). It does seem odd that the *wives* of a church officer must also have certain qualifications if they themselves do not serve in the office. And we must ask why *deacons'* wives have to be respectable, temperate, etc., but the wives of *overseers* go unmentioned. This leads to the second view.

The interpretation of 3:11 represented in the NIV margin translation ("deaconesses") takes the *gynaikes* here as female deacons alongside males. This would explain why Paul mentions them in the middle of his list of deacon quali-fications. The absence of a reference to "women" in the overseer section is now explicable (cf. 2:9–15). Paul is not legis-lating the qualifications for the wives of church officers in 3:11, but of female deacons. If this is so, why then didn't Paul simply clear up matters by saying *deaconesses* in 3:11 instead of the more ambiguous "women"? The answer is that Greek did not have a separate word for "deaconess" at that time. The same Greek word *diakonos* (from which we get "deacon" in English) was used to refer to either male or female "deacons" (accompanied by either the masculine or feminine article to express the gender of the noun when required). In other words, Paul had no real choice, so his use of "women" was as clear as anything to designate women deacons.

In either case, Paul specifies a high ethical standard for the women of 3:11, similar to the standards for overseers and deacons. The behavior code in 3:1–13 is not different from the ethical requirement for any Christian, but church officers should particularly exemplify these

▶Deaconesses in Early Church History

In A.D. 110, Pliny the Younger reported to the Emperor Trajan that he has examined Christians in his province of Bithynia (a Roman province north of Ephesus) to discover the nature of their presumed criminal activities and only found a harmless cult. He continues, "This made me decide it was all the more necessary to extract the truth by torture from two slave-women [*ancillae*], whom they call deaconesses [*ministrae*]."[A-7] We should note: (1) These women were slaves, and it was customary for Roman officials to interrogate slaves (but not others) under torture; (2) the women were called "deaconesses" by the Christians (Latin *ministrae* is the equivalent of Greek *diakonoi*). In other words, this seems to be an official title, not a generic reference to their being "servants" of some sort, since we already know them to have been "slaves" (*ancillae*). Hence, this suggests that the church had female deacons within forty or fifty years of the writing of 1 Timothy—perhaps women like Phoebe, "a servant [*diakonos*] of the church in Cenchrea" (Rom. 16:1).[A-8]

high qualities for the sake of "God's household" (3:15), even though they enjoy immunity from casual charges of wrongdoing (5:19).

Paul's Plans (3:14–16)

I hope to come to you soon (3:14). Paul hoped to visit Timothy and the church of Ephesus (and probably of surrounding cities) soon. Paul did not know when he would be able to make this proposed trip, and we do not know whether he actually made the trip. Subsequently, he was on trial in Rome at the writing of 2 Timothy, and we may suspect that Paul himself was unsure of his freedom of movement when he tells Timothy that he hopes to visit Ephesus soon.

The pillar and foundation of the truth (3:15). Paul had a high regard for the church since he calls it "the pillar and foundation of the truth." In this remarkable statement, he uses a building analogy, which would have spoken strongly to someone living in first-century Ephesus. This city was experiencing a remarkable building program, some of them of massive proportions. The temple of the city goddess, Artemis Ephesia, was

the largest temple building in antiquity and one of the seven wonders of the ancient world. Its elaborately carved columns and foundation stones were of monumental size, which was particularly prized in a region that often suffered devastating earthquakes.

He appeared in a body (3:16). Paul appears to quote a brief summary of the truths of the gospel here, perhaps used to instruct people before their baptism. In many church services today the Apostles' or Nicene Creeds are recited regularly in worship services as testimony to the historic Christian faith. Paul could have been the author of this wonderful summary of the work of Christ, or he could

PILLAR AND FOUNDATION

The foundation of the temple of Apollo at Delphi. ▼

REFLECTIONS

IN OUR PLURALISTIC AGE, THE universal church's role as the "pillar and foundation of the truth" is under direct and indirect assault, even from "church" people. Some refuse communion and membership with any church, or they carelessly roam from church to church without ever making any lasting commitment. In the scholarly realm, some evangelical theologians question whether faith in Christ is indeed required to enjoy eternal life, making church membership even more irrelevant and ultimately absurd. But God himself claims to be the patriarchal head of his "household" (3:15), and he takes this role seriously—so seriously that he gave his only Son to purchase his adopted family by his own blood. Not even hell itself and all of its devices will eventually overcome her and God's truth (Matt. 16:18; cf. 1 Tim. 4:1).

be passing on what had already become a traditional summary. In any case, in this verse one can see the historical work of Christ at the heart of Paul's gospel.

Warning about False Teaching (4:1–5)

Paul follows up his teaching on the qualifications of church officers in chapter 3 with specific warnings about false doctrine "in later times" (4:1), which Timothy himself will encounter since the whole era between the first and second coming of Christ is the "last hour" (1 John 2:18). Paul ends this chapter with some positive instructions for Timothy's public ministry (1 Tim. 4:6–16).

Things taught by demons (4:1). Paul is not concerned here with paganism per se, but with false teaching within the church. These false teachers have "abandoned the faith" they once embraced in order to follow demonic doctrines. The word "demon" (Gk. *daimonion*; plural *daimonia*) to ancient ears would not necessarily sound evil. Indeed, the pagan Greeks used to pour out a libation of wine to *Agathos Daemon* ("Good Demon"), who was, interestingly, represented in works of art by a snake. And Paul's original readers were accustomed to hearing about *daimonia* teaching and guiding people through oracles, prophecy, or in other ways. For instance, it was generally thought that the prophetic god Apollo used *daimonia* as agents for the oracles at Delphi on mainland Greece or at Didyma in Asia Minor. Socrates, the famous philosopher, claimed to be personally guided by such a *daimonion*, leading to ancient speculation on the identity of this being.[39] In contrast, Paul says that the Holy Spirit himself has *expressly* provided a warning against the teaching of *daimonia*, which are deceiving spirits (see also 1 John 4:1–3).

Whose consciences have been seared (4:2). Apostate teachers can wantonly betray their Lord because their "consciences have been seared as with a hot iron." This arresting analogy is clear in any culture, but it was particularly vivid in antiquity where penal branding took place. An inscription found in the vicinity of Ephesus threatens branding (possibly on the foot) as punishment for seditious bakers who had been instigating local riots (*IvE* 215). Closer to Paul's image, runaway slaves who were recaptured might have their foreheads branded by harsh masters (Apuleius, *Golden Ass* 9; 3 *Macc.* 2:29).[40]

They forbid people to marry and order them to abstain from certain foods (4:3). The apostle identifies asceticism as the particular subject that characterizes the teaching of liars. Paul was no gourmand objecting to the disapproval of delicacies. His argument strikes against the substitution of Christianity's true focal point of "love, which comes from a pure heart and a good conscience and a sincere faith" (1:5) with an empty ascetic exhibitionism (Col. 2:20–23). The rejection of monogamous marriage was not common among ancient peoples. Both the Greeks and Romans had high ideals of marriage, particularly for the purpose of childbearing and securing the family line.

For everything God created is good (4:4). Paul alludes to his rationale for holding foods and marriage in high esteem by referring to God's creation of these good things. After making the produce of sea and land God saw that it was "good" and later that all his creation, including the union of Adam with Eve, was "very good" (Gen. 1:20–21, 31). The ascetics do not sin against the gifts themselves, but against the Giver of every good and perfect gift (James 1:17) by contradicting and disbelieving his Word. Ambrosiaster, the name given to an unknown church father, wrote: "Why, then, do some people call that which God has blessed a sordid and contaminated work, unless because they themselves in some way raise their hands against God? For they would not criticize this [work], unless they had wicked ideas about God, the Maker of the work."[41] That God's good provisions in creation are not "to be rejected" but to be received with thanksgiving (1 Tim. 4:4) finds an interesting verbal parallel in Homer's *Iliad*, the closest thing to the Bible among the ancient Greeks: "The glorious gifts of the gods are never *to be rejected*."[42]

Training in Godliness (4:6–10)

The importance of the objective "truths of the faith and of the good teaching" must not be overlooked. (The word "teaching" or "doctrine" occurs four times in this chapter alone.) Timothy will be a "good minister" or servant of Christ if he conveys these things faithfully. But the reward for his faithfulness for himself and others is to be "brought up" on these things, or better, *nourished* by these things. Pure teaching of Christian doctrine, rather than being deadening for our spiritual life, is food for the soul.[43]

In stark contrast to the excellent doctrine stands the degrading myths of Timothy's contemporaries (cf. 1 Tim. 1:3–4). Rape, adultery, murder, lying, deceit, and trickery of every sort pervade the activities of the gods in ancient mythology. Many pagans thought that there might be an historical core to the myths, but that the poets and playwrights had added many embarrassing embellishments:[44] "The poets tell many lies" was a common ancient saying. Plato rather disdainfully rejected such myths from the educational program in his ideal republic.[45]

Physical training is of some value (4:8). "Physical training" would be familiar to Timothy. The Greek word for "training"

▶ Asceticism in Antiquity

Asceticism of various sorts was known in the New Testament world, though one must admit that its practitioners are found on the fringe of New Testament societies and their vital thought. Vegetarianism was taught by some Greek philosophical schools active in the first century, especially the Neopythagoreans and the Cynics. There were ascetic cult groups such as the followers of Cybele, who was served by emasculated priests. The latter, "a howling rabble" thumping drums and clashing cymbals, were suspected of being mere religious hucksters by some people.[A-9] Chaeremon the Stoic (one of Nero's tutors) is said by Porphyry to have described the ascetic lives of Egyptian temple priests who rejected various foods and practiced sexual abstinence (though not necessarily rejection of marriage itself). Likewise the Shrine of Heracles the Misogynist in Phocis required that annual priests had to remain chaste during their year of service. Plutarch comments: "For this reason they usually appoint as priests rather old men."[A-10] Josephus relates the Essene community's rejection of marriage because "it leads to domestic quarrels."[A-11] Some later heretical Christian groups like the Marcionites, Montanists, and Manichaeans taught asceticism in various forms.[A-12]

is *gymnasia* and is the source of our "gymnasium." There was no institution more characteristic of Hellenic culture than the gymnasium, where youths in schools were subjected to a rigorous course of athletics.[46] In earlier times, the gymnasium was essential for military training, since a city-state's army consisted of all male citizens. By NT times, a few noble Greeks might enter the Roman army, but most athletics in the gymnasium—aside from the numerous professional athletes and their guilds—had degenerated into the practice of "body sculpting." The Romans did not always go in for this, as Plutarch (a first-century Greek) explains:

> For the Romans used to be very suspicious of rubbing down with oil, and even today they believe that nothing has been so much to blame for the enslavement and effeminacy of the Greeks as their gymnasia and wrestling-schools, which engender much listless idleness and waste of time in their cities, as well as pederasty and the ruin of the bodies of the young men with regulated sleeping, walking, rhythmical movements, and strict diet; by these practices they have unconsciously lapsed from the practice of arms, and have become content to be termed nimble athletes and handsome wrestlers. (Plutarch, *Roman Questions*, 40; LCL translation)

The living God, who is the Savior (4:10). In first-century society, the word "savior" was familiar as the title of gods, emperors, provincial governors, and other patrons who provided certain *earthly benefactions* to communities or individuals in time of need. "Savior" was virtually synonymous with "benefactor." This can be easily substantiated, but an inscription from Ephesus illustrates this point by using the two words in parallel. The guild of silversmiths honored a provincial governor as "their own savior and benefactor in all things."[47]

One especially important example of "savior" relating to earthly benefactions comes from a recovered statue base inscription from Ephesus, which Timothy may have seen many times by the time he read this letter—recall that it was received at Ephesus (1:3). The statue was erected in honor of Julius Caesar in 48 B.C. after he had saved the province from financial ruin. The inscription reads: "The

REFLECTIONS

WE CAN SEE FROM 1 TIMOTHY 4:8 that Paul had no real enthusiasm for gymnastic training for his young Greek friend Timothy. He does, however, wholeheartedly endorse training in *godliness*, which—what a marvelous thought!—"has value for all things, holding promise for both the present life and the life to come." The sculpted body will wither and die, but not the godly character of God's children!

GYMNASIUM

The remains of the gymnasium at Laodicea.

▼

cities of Asia, along with the [citizen-bodies] and the nations, (honor) C. Julius C. f. Caesar, Pontifex Maximus, Emperor, and twice Consul, *the manifest god* (sprung) from Ares and Aphrodite, and *universal savior of human life"* (*IvE* 251; emphasis added). Both Caesar's divine honors and the "savior" title are of interest, for, in contrast, Paul says that we have set our hope in a *living God*—not this long-dead "manifest god"—and that our living God is the true benefactor of even these misguided pagans, "and especially of those who believe." In other words, Paul's statement in 4:10 has a polemical side effect in its original context.[48]

The Character of Timothy's Public Ministry (4:11–16)

Young pastors everywhere have taken encouragement from 4:11–12. In both the Roman and the Greek world, social and political leadership belonged to older men. The Latin word *senate* comes from *senex*, "old, senior." At Athens and other Hellenic cities like Ephesus, there was a

semiofficial body of elders, the *Gerousia* (from Gk., *geron*, "old man"), which played an important role in politics, religion, and society. Elders played a key role in the church also, and we read about "the elders" of Ephesus in Acts 20:17.[49]

In this ancient climate, one can appreciate Timothy's delicate position as a leader in the church. He is told to "*command* and teach these things," even to people who were senior to him in age. This might lead to pride, but the guard against this is found at the end of 4:12: The young pastor is to execute his office in an exemplary fashion with love and purity. To minister like this from the heart will naturally foster humility. A teacher is a *servant*.

The public reading of Scripture (4:13). Notice here how central the Word of God is to Timothy's ministry. He is to *devote* himself to its public reading, proclamation, and teaching. We take the Bible for granted today. In Timothy's day, even though books were widely available (2 Tim. 4:13), they were expensive, and not everyone could read. Thus the public reading and proclamation of the Word was especially vital for the health of the church. It was so important that God gave a special attestation of Timothy's ordination to this ministry "through a prophetic message" when the "body of elders" (Gk. *presbyteros*) laid their hands on him. This body was probably the Ephesian group whom Paul addressed in nearby Miletus (Acts 20:17). There were no religions in antiquity as "bookish" as Christianity except Judaism (e.g., Acts 15:21).

Be diligent in these matters (4:15). The young pastor is to be especially diligent and watchful both in his progress in sanctification and in his doctrine. Life and

▶

AN OLDER MAN

Roman statue of an older man.

doctrine must never be separated in either the minister or in the church. They are the guarantee of perseverance in our holy faith, leading to salvation "both for yourself and your hearers."

Timothy's Ministry to Various Groups (5:1–2)

Paul instructs Timothy on his relations with others within the Christian community and, one would expect by implication, on how he should also deal with non-Christians. In 5:1–2, he summarizes Timothy's relations with both men and women, older and younger. This shows that the early Christians were drawn from a broad cross-section within their society, not from any one subgroup only (cf. 1 John 2:12–14).

Ministry to Widows (5:3–8)

Most of 1 Timothy 5 is taken up with how Timothy should administer and relate to widows. The obvious point is that there were enough widows in the early church in the Ephesus area for Timothy to be charged with this task, which could consume a substantial portion of the church's resources (cf. Acts 6:1–4).[50]

Those widows who are really in need (5:3). Widowhood could be a severe test in the Greco-Roman world, since women were usually not the direct heirs of their husband's wills. Rather, the widow had her dowry as well as any stipulation that the testator made for her care to his heirs (usually the male children of the marriage). If the son or sons did not care for their mother (or often, their stepmother), the woman could be in a dire condition if her dowry was not substantial (hence, Paul's stern statement in 5:8).[51] One Greek will from the mid-second century, for instance, leaves all the property to the son, but the use and income of the property went to the man's wife for the duration of her life (P.Oxy. 494). But this was not always the case, especially among the poor.

We should add that men outlived women in antiquity. Research has shown that the average life expectancy for women who survived childhood in the Hellenistic period was about thirty-six years and for men between forty-two and forty-five years. The difference is explained as the result of a high mortality rate of mothers during childbirth.[52]

The widow who lives for pleasure (5:6). Not all widows were obviously in desperate need. The wealthy widow could occupy her time in vain entertainments. For instance, read this reference in the younger Pliny regarding the later years of a socially prominent Roman matron:

> Ummidia Quadratilla is dead, having almost attained the age of seventy-nine and kept her powers unimpaired up to her last illness, along with a sound constitution and sturdy physique which are rare in a woman. . . . She kept a troupe of pantomime actors whom she treated with an indulgence unsuitable in a lady of her high position. . . . Once when she was asking me to supervise her grandson's education she told me that as a woman, with all a woman's idle hours to fill, she was in the habit of amusing herself playing draughts or watching her mimes.[53]

The Widow List (5:9–16)

Paul now turns his attention to the church's ministry to certain formally recognized widows. There was apparently a list kept by the church for the care of widows (cf. Acts 6:1 again), who were committed to staying single and providing certain services in return (care for children, hospitality, washing the feet of the saints, and other "good deeds"). These widows would pledge themselves to this arrangement for the duration of their life—hence Paul's restriction for younger widows to serve Christ in the church in this way (5:11–12). (Other-

wise, Paul seems to contradict himself by criticizing younger widows for wanting to remarry in 5:11–12 and then telling them to remarry in 5:14.) In this way, these older saints who had no earthly family support were provided for in "God's household" (3:15), and they themselves could actively serve the saints in some way. The tasks they carried out may appear humble, but when carried out as a pledge to Christ (5:11) like the "widow's mite," they were undoubtedly a sweet savor to the Lord (cf. 5:24–25).

Instructions on Elders and Other Matters (5:17–25)

Paul now addresses particular treatment of the elders of the congregation. He had specified the qualifications for this office earlier, and now he gives some passing information about their office ("direct[ing] the affairs of the church" and especially "preaching and teaching") as well as some instructions about their financial support (implied in the "double honor," which is their due). Much has been written lately in scholarly literature about the social significance of honor and shame in Mediterranean societies of antiquity. This is particularly important for understanding the Corinthian correspondence, but we also see it here in Paul's reference to "double honors" for elders (cf. the fifth commandment: "*Honor* your father and your mother . . ."). See the accompanying box for an example of public honor at Ephesus.[54]

Ephesus and other Greek cities of the time had a body of elders, called the *Gerousia*, at the time (see above on 4:11–16). The elders of the church do not really correspond to this group in every way, but like the elders of the Jewish synagogue, they show the important gov-

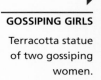

GOSSIPING GIRLS

Terracotta statue of two gossiping women.

R E F L E C T I O N S

PAUL, APPLYING THE FIFTH COMMANDMENT, SAYS that the one who neglects to care for his relatives "has denied the faith and is worse than an unbeliever" (5:8). This is strong language indeed, so we must carefully heed its message today, especially in our day of fragmented families. Divorce and widowhood plagued families in the first century; however, there were usually no governmental institutions to substitute for the family and short-circuit it as there are now. It was not unusual for a household in antiquity to include a widowed sister or aunt and the cousins.[A-13] And it was normal for elderly parents to join the household, for there were no rest homes or care centers in antiquity. Paul's instructions show just how vital the home is as a fundamental, divinely-ordained social institution.

ernmental role of older men in the social and religious life of the ancient communities. We cannot stress enough that religion, society, and politics were not separate spheres in antiquity as they are today. Hence the public priests, court officials, fathers of the clans, and city council members were normally one small group of older men in the city.

Use a little wine (5:23). This verse comes as a surprise to some people today because they are convinced that the Bible teaches total abstinence from alcoholic liquor. They may take the "wine" here to refer to grape juice, but that is not likely, since all wine used in antiquity was alcoholic. Without refrigeration or chemical preservatives, grape juice quickly turns to vinegar, whereas fermentation of wine was a form of preservation. Wine was alcoholic but not necessarily intoxicating, since the ancients regularly mixed their wine with varying parts of water.

The really surprising thing in 5:23 is that Paul advises Timothy to drink wine at *Ephesus*. The wine produced there was notoriously bad. The elder Pliny, who wrote a whole section of his *Natural History* (better thought of as a "Miscellany") on the different wines around in the mid-first century A.D., says: "As for the vintage of Mesogis, it has been found to cause headaches, and that of Ephesus has also proved to be unwholesome, because sea-water and boiled must [grape juice before it has fermented] are employed to season it."[55] Sea-water! It must have been wretched stuff, but Paul hopes that it will ward off Timothy's "frequent illnesses."

The sins of others trail behind them . . . good deeds are obvious (5:24–25). Paul ends this chapter with resumption of the thought from 5:22 about the sins of some, then concludes with the public character of good deeds. Life in the Mediterranean cities was (and is) a public life. With

---

▶ **The Quest for Public Honors**

One example of the demand for public honor in antiquity comes in the form of an inscribed letter from the Emperor Antoninus Pius to the Ephesian city fathers (Ephesus, A.D. 145). What is most remarkable about this letter is that the recipient had it inscribed in stone on a public building (which he financed) in order for all to see.

Titus Aelius Hadrian Antoninus Pius . . . to the rulers, the council, and the people of the Ephesians, greetings. I did not learn about the generosity which Vedius Antoninus shows you from your letters but from his. Because, wishing to enlist my help for the adornment of the public works which he promised you, he showed me how many and what magnificent buildings he is adding to the city. But you do not appreciate him properly [i.e., you have not given him enough public honors]. I, for my part, have granted him all that he requested. I appreciated that he hopes to make the city more august in a manner (looking) to the (future?), not following the fashion of many public figures who expend their generosity on spectacles, on distributions, and on prizes for the games (only) for the sake of immediate popularity (*IvE* 1491).

▶

EPHESUS

Terraced homes for
the wealthy citizens
of Ephesus. This has
been a key focus of
the archaeological
excavations.

cramped houses stacked one on top of another and with narrow, winding streets, people spent their lives openly before their neighbors. What was done in the home was soon known in the market-places, so that even good deeds that are not obvious "cannot be hidden."

Slaves' Obedience to Their Masters (6:1–2)

Galen, the second-century A.D. medical writer, estimated that one-third of the population of Pergamum in Asia Minor were slaves. Modern scholars usually believe that this figure may even be too low for cities like Ephesus, Athens, or Rome, so the issue of slavery was practical and important for Paul to address.

Ancient slavery was a variegated phenomenon. Private slaves could be found in great misery grinding flour in chains at a mill, or in relative prosperity working on their own in small businesses, hardly different in most respects from their free neighbors except that all of their profits were at the disposal of their masters. Public slaves could be important government officials or menial attendants in the public baths. Slaves and freedmen (freed slaves) were everywhere, and few households did not have one or more maids and slave boys to do the household chores, cooking, and gardening. Essayists of the time expounded on the humanity of slaves and the essential equality of slave and free, but this sort of thing was an exercise in rhetoric or philosophy and had no practical effect on ancient slavery.[56]

Paul's instructions on the respectful attitude of slaves toward their masters

REFLECTIONS

PAUL WRITES THAT SLAVES MUST obey willingly as testimony to the power of the gospel. Today's Western societies do not have debt bondage or slavery. However by extension, Paul's instructions do apply to our relations with "all those in authority" over us (2:2).

comes against the backdrop of a standard theme in ancient comedies: the arrogant, back-talking slave. Over and over the Greek and Latin comic playwrights present slaves as mocking their masters behind their backs, talking back to them with barely disguised contempt when they could (often getting a cuffing for comic effect), and generally being villainous characters. Admittedly a large measure of this picture was simply the comedic portrait, but it no doubt contains an element of truth, especially when read in light of more direct historical sources.[57]

Godliness and Gain (6:3–10)

If anyone teaches false doctrines (6:3). In our day, good doctrine in a teacher often takes a back seat to charismatic stage presence. It is only natural, but such teachers sometimes lead people and churches to ruin. It was no different in the early centuries of the Christian church, as Paul indicates. Notice how he emphasizes "sound instruction," which can more literally be rendered "healthy" or "health-giving" instruction and which is contrasted with the "gangrenous" doctrine of heretics (2 Tim. 2:17). The evil doctrine of false teachers goes hand in glove with their evil and self-serving character.

Godliness with contentment is great gain (6:6). The avarice of the false teachers brings Paul to express some classic thoughts:

- "We brought nothing into the world, and we can take nothing out of it."

> ## ▶ Portrait of a False Teacher
>
> Unfortunately, we can read about many quack teachers in the history of Christianity, but one of the more interesting is a fellow named Peregrinus of Parium in the region of Propontis (near the Hellespont). Peregrinus is interesting because a vivid portrait of this huckster was drawn in an essay by the second century A.D. humorist Lucian of Samosata (the Mark Twain or Garrison Keillor of antiquity). According to Lucian, Peregrinus had the following encounter in the church while running from the law:
>
> It was then that he learned the wondrous lore of the Christians, by associating with their priests and scribes in Palestine. And—how else could it be?—in a trice he made them all look like children; for he was prophet, cult-leader, head of the synagogue, and everything, all by himself. He interpreted and explained some of their books and even composed many, and they revered him as a god, made use of him as a lawgiver, and set him down as a protector ("On the Death of Peregrinus" 11; LCL trans.).
>
> Peregrinus was soon apprehended by the anti-Christian authorities—who were actually fairly tolerant in this period, so he must have made himself odious to them—and he was thrown into prison. The Christians both in Palestine and as far away as Asia Minor were said to have spared no expense helping Peregrinus in his imprisonment so that "he procured not a little revenue from it" and afterward lived "in unalloyed prosperity" off the church. Lucian thinks the Christians to be very gullible; he writes, "So if any charlatan and trickster, able to profit by occasions, comes among them, he quickly acquires sudden wealth by imposing upon simple folk" ("On the Death of Peregrinus" 13). In any case, Peregrinus soon apostatized from Christianity and became a Cynic philosopher. He made a sensational exit by immolating himself at the Olympic games in A.D. 165. Paul's warning against and characterization of false teachers finds clear points of contact with Peregrinus and many others afterward.

"For the love of money is a root of all kinds of evil."

Root of all kinds of evil (6:10). No one in any society loves a grasping, avaricious individual. Such types were the brunt of frequent lampoons by the comic playwrights and essayists in antiquity. The student and successor of the philosopher Aristotle was a man named Theophrastus, who wrote a work called "Characters," or better, "Character Traits." Four of his thirty sketches center on character flaws connected to money: "Sponging," "Pennypinching," "Lack of Generosity," and "Chiseling." The modern reader who reads these 2300-year-old portraits of defective characters will find many familiar themes and confirm Paul's statement about money being at the root of broken friendships, shattered marriages, a bad reputation, and all kinds of evil.

The Good Fight (6:11–16)

Fight the good fight of the faith (6:12). The background of the "good fight of the faith" is war. Wars were brewing on the horizon in Palestine at the time Paul wrote 1 Timothy, which eventually broke out in the Jewish revolt and all the horrible atrocities of which the Roman army was capable.[58] Otherwise, the Roman empire was relatively peaceful except on its faraway borders, where skirmishes with wandering barbarian tribes often took place. Timothy's fight is to be one "of the faith," which will confirm that his public confession of faith was genuine and thereby guarantee that he is indeed a holder of the

▶ "If We Have Food"

The staple foods in Asia Minor at the time of Timothy were bread, olive oil, fish (on the seacoasts), and wine. Sometimes one would enjoy meat after public sacrifices (usually oxen or pork) or a fowl. Some staples that the modern world takes for granted (e.g., potatoes, corn [maize], squash, and tomatoes) originated from the Americas and were not present in Europe until after Columbus. The ancients ate vegetables and fruits, but only in season, since food preservation was primitive though not entirely unknown. Meat and fish were usually salted (or stored in a jar of honey), otherwise meats especially had to be used right away because there was no refrigeration.

The wealthy, of course, ate sumptuously because they could afford it.[A-14] We possess an ancient Roman cookbook by a man named Apicius, which has happily been translated and edited by a man who was both a chef and a Latin scholar.[A-15] This cookbook contains some extravagant recipes like boiled ostrich, brains and bacon, and seafood minced with sea-onion, lovage, pepper, cumin, and laser root, as well as more mundane dishes like barley broth, wine sauces, and a sardine omelet. Most people in antiquity in the Mediterranean area, however, ate a basic diet of bread dipped in wine or oil and a dried fish now and then. Such a diet did not always lead to disease prevention and longevity.

eternal life he is to preach (6:12). It is a fight against evil, and its weapons are characterized by righteousness, godliness, love, and gentleness.[59]

God . . . the King of kings and Lord of lords (6:15). By ascribing to God the title "King of kings and Lord of lords" (titles ascribed to Christ in Rev. 17:14; 19:16), Paul uses language that was common in his day. The Roman emperors were technically not "kings," for the Romans were traditionally antiregal after they had overthrown the last of the old Tarquinian kings (see comments on 1 Tim. 2:2). But they were regularly given this title in the provinces, as we find in the Gospels (e.g., John 19:15), where local rulers like the Herods were styled "kings" (e.g., Matt. 14:9). But everyone in the Roman world knew what a king was, and now some of the Gentiles knew the "King of kings."

◄ RELIEF OF EPHESIAN GLADIATORS

▶ Violence and Greek Athletics

It is commonly assumed that the brutal Roman gladiatorial games were practiced in Greece and Asia Minor in Paul's day, but I have my doubts that this is true. There is evidence for gladiatorial contests in Asia Minor in the second century A.D., but not in Paul's day fifty or sixty years earlier. There was no initial enthusiasm for these bloody affairs in the Greek world, and the Greeks had a long tradition of games of their own, which they were reluctant to give up or modify. In part this is because the Greek games were connected to religious rites. To change the contests in the games meant a virtual change of religion or even a possible violation of religious principles for the Greeks. For instance, to spill blood in contests before a sacrifice was sometimes thought to usurp the effectiveness of the attendant blood sacrifice and to offend the gods.

On the other hand, Greek athletics were sometimes brutal enough without gladiators. Boxing was regularly performed with leather straps bound across the athlete's hands to protect his knuckles. You can imagine that this gave no padding for the blows on the opponent. (Boxers sometimes used padded gloves in practice, however.) It was normal for boxers to receive grievous wounds, and the Greek Anthology (11.75) even contains a story about a boxer who was disinherited because he no longer resembled his portrait painted earlier in life; he could not prove his identity from the portrait because of his battered features. Even more dangerous than boxing was the Greek pankration event, which seems to resemble oriental martial arts or kick boxing because the boxers were allowed to use their feet to kick and to trip their opponent. Even without gladiators the Greek world of the first century certainly witnessed plenty of fighting.

**TEMPLE TREASURY
AT DELPHI**

God, who richly provides us with everything for our enjoyment (6:17). The expression "sinfully delicious" today dishonors God. If something is delicious, it is because God has made it so for our thankful enjoyment. We should give him thanks for this and for all of his other good gifts, because they are good. However, this does not mean that we should practice hedonism (a word derived from the Greek word for "pleasure"). The hedonists of Paul's day were the followers of Epicureus (cf. Acts 17:18), though gluttony and other idolatrous practices were commonplace enough among ancient peoples who had no philosophical pretensions.

What is falsely called knowledge (6:20). Paul concludes this letter with a final warning to hold fast to the gospel and to reject "godless chatter" and false teaching—"what is falsely called knowledge" and leads directly out of the church's doors. By referring to this teaching as so-called "knowledge," Paul may be referring to a trend that developed in later decades into a collection of heretical teachings now known as "Gnosticism" (from Gk. *gnōsis*, "knowledge"). This widespread movement was not connected with only one teacher, group, or location (though the main evidence for it comes from Egypt[60]). Gnosticism was to become a major threat to the orthodoxy of the Christian church.

R E F L E C T I O N S

VARIOUS GROUPS IN THE EARLY CHURCH HAD A common denominator that is still a massive temptation today, namely, to focus on some *secret* or *special* knowledge available only to a select group in the church, which sets them above all the rest of the "common herd." Paul does not condemn the true knowledge of God or of the "sound instruction" (6:3) that he himself taught. But such secret, so-called knowledge is not only false knowledge of God, it is destructive to the unity of the faith and the bond of love that must typify the Christian community (e.g., 1 Cor. 8:1–3; Eph. 4:3).

Dibelius, Martin, and Hans Conzelmann. *The Pastoral Epistles.* Hermeneia. Philadelphia: Fortress, 1972.

This critical commentary relies on the typical reasons for rejecting Pauline authorship of the Pastorals, but helpfully gives detailed attention to the historical background and especially connections of the Pastoral Letters with the Hellenistic world.

Fee, Gordon D. *1 and 2 Timothy, Titus.* GNC. San Francisco: Harper & Row, 1984.

This is a concise commentary by a well-regarded NT and text-critical scholar in a popular format.

Guthrie, Donald. *The Pastoral Epistles: An Introduction and Commentary.* TNTC. Leicester and Grand Rapids: InterVarsity and Eerdmans, 1990 (rev. ed.).

A solid though brief commentary by a senior evangelical NT scholar.

Kelly, J. N. D. *A Commentary on the Pastoral Epistles.* TC. London: A. & C. Black, 1963; reprinted Grand Rapids: Baker, 1981.

This brief commentary sticks closely to the text and is marked by Kelly's characteristic sound judgment. Kelly is well versed in original sources and has produced a number of standard works in the later development of early Christianity, which add depth to his commentary.

Kidd, Reggie M. *Wealth and Beneficence in the Pastoral Epistles: A "Bourgeois" Form of Early Christianity?* Atlanta: Scholars, 1990.

This is the best of many such studies on the contemporary social and ethical background of the Pastoral Letters. Kidd surveys an extensive range of background material in this work.

Knight, George W. III. *Commentary on the Pastoral Epistles.* NIGTC. Grand Rapids and Carlisle: Eerdmans and Paternoster, 1992.

This detailed commentary on the Greek text of the Pastorals often gives illuminating historical insights as well as careful attention to the meaning of the grammar and language of the biblical text. The best technical commentary on the Pastorals in print today.

Lau, Andrew L. *Manifest in Flesh: The Epiphany Christology of the Pastoral Epistles.* WUNT 2/86. Tübingen: J. C. B. Mohr (Paul Siebeck), 1996.

This specialized study draws especially helpful connections between the epiphany material in the Pastorals with the OT and other Jewish literature.

Oden, Thomas C. *First and Second Timothy and Titus.* Interpretation. Louisville: John Knox, 1989.

Oden presents an elegant and sane defense of Pauline authorship in this topically arranged "commentary." There are a few rough spots regarding historical background of the biblical world (e.g., sacred prostitution at Ephesus, p. 95), but Oden augments his own helpful insights with a sprinkling of quotations of church fathers and Reformers, which gives the reader a wider view of the interpretation of the Pastoral Letters.

Young, Frances. *The Theology of the Pastoral Letters.* NTT. Cambridge: Cambridge Univ. Press, 1994.

This volume in a promising series spends considerable time trying to establish pseudonymous authorship of the Pastorals. Nevertheless, Young usefully reports on historical backgrounds of the Pastorals in places—for instance, on "teaching and learning in the ancient world" (pp. 79–84), though it seems mostly secondary and derivative.

CHAPTER NOTES

Main Text Notes

1. Cf. E. R. Richards, *The Secretary in the Letters of Paul* (WUNT 2.42; Tübingen: J. C. B. Mohr [Paul Siebeck], 1991). For indications of Paul's use of a secretary see 1 Cor. 16:21; Gal. 6:11; Col. 4:18; 2 Thess. 3:17; Philem. 19.

2. Isocrates stated the ancient view well: "The birthright of a liberal education is marked not by courage, wealth and similar distinctions, but most clearly of all by speech, the sign which presents the most reliable proof of education" (in M. Grant, ed., *Greek Literature: An Anthology* [London: Penguin, 1977], 225); see especially the classic: H. I. Marrou, *A History of Education in Antiquity* (New York: Sheed and Ward, 1956).

3. Josephus, *Ag. Ap.* 1.9 §50; H. St. J. Thackeray in his introduction to *Josephus* (LCL; Cambridge, Mass.: Harvard Univ. Press, 1926), 1:xiii.

4. For brief and helpful treatments on the authorship issue see E. E. Ellis, "Pastoral Letters," *DPL*, 658–66; D. A. Carson, Douglas J. Moo, and Leon Morris, *An Introduction to the New Testament* (Grand Rapids: Zondervan, 1992), 359–71; George W. Knight III, *The Pastoral Epistles: A Commentary on the Greek Text* (NIGTC; Grand Rapids and Carlisle: Eerdmans and Paternoster, 1992), 4–52.

5. Richards, *The Secretary in Paul's Letters*, 193; cf. 53–56.

6. The *SC Turpilianum*, Tacitus, *Ann.* 14.41; Harry W. Tajra, *The Trial of St. Paul* (WUNT 35; Tübingen: J. C. B. Mohr, 1989), 194.

7. See Tajra's remarks, *Trial of St. Paul*, 196.

8. Philo, *Moses* 1.15.

9. Philo, *Spec. Laws* 4.203.

10. P.Lips. 28; A.D. 381.

11. Strabo 14.1.24

12. Ignatius, *Ephesians* 1.3.

13. See H. Büchsel, "γενεαλογία," *TDNT*, 1:662–65.

14. *Magnesians* 8:1; cf. *Polycarp* 3:1; *Smyrnaeans* 6:2.

15. Polybius 9.2.1.

16. Polybius 9.1.1; LCL trans.

17. See Plutarch's *Solon* for an ancient biography.

18. Plato, *Apology*.

19. The play is ascribed to Seneca, but this is not accepted today. The quoted line is from E. F. Watling, trans., *Seneca: Four Tragedies and Octavia* (Baltimore: Penguin, 1966), 280.

20. See also Titus 1:3; cf. 1 Cor. 9:17; Gal. 2:7.

21. For a good discussion of these passages see George W. Knight, III, *The Faithful Sayings in the Pastoral Letters* (Nutley, N.J.: Presbyterian & Reformed, n.d.); see also 3:1; 4:9; 2 Tim. 2:11; Titus 3:8.

22. Cf. Matt. 9:13; Luke 5:32; 19:10; John 3:17; 12:46–47.

23. See also Ps. 115:1; Luke 2:14; Rom. 11:36; 16:27; Gal. 1:5; Eph. 3:21; Phil. 4:20; 2 Tim. 4:18; Heb. 13:21; 2 Peter 3:18; Jude 25; Rev. 1:6; 4:11; 5:12–13; 7:12.

24. E.g., 2 Cor. 10:4; Eph. 6:11–17; 1 Tim. 6:12; 2 Tim. 4:7.

25. E.g., Josephus, *J.W.* 3.8.3 §351.

26. Rom. 3:29–30; cf. Gal. 3:20; Eph. 4:5–6.

27. The standard work is Leon Morris, *The Apostolic Preaching of the Cross* (Grand Rapids: Eerdmans, 1955; now in subsequent editions).

28. E.g., *IvE* 687, 724, 1004, 1687.

29. Ps. 28:2; cf. Lam. 2:19; 3:41–42; Ps. 134:2; cf. 63:4; 119:48; emphasis added in each case.

30. For further reading see S. M. Baugh, "A Foreign World: Ephesus in the First Century," in *Women in the Church: A Fresh Analysis of 1 Timothy 2:9–15* (eds. A. Köstenberger, T. Schreiner, and H. S. Baldwin; Grand Rapids: Baker, 1995), 13–52.

31. *Ephesian Story* 1.2; see B. P. Reardon, ed., *Collected Ancient Greek Novels* (Berkeley: Univ. of California Press, 1989), 129.

32. Cf. Plutarch, "Advice to Bride and Groom" (*Moralia* 141E), for a similar commendation for a woman's adornment in her character rather than in her dress; Ignatius, *Ephesians* 9.2.

33. E.g., Shepherd of Hermas, *Similitudes* 9.9.5.

34. For more on this subject and sources see Baugh, "Foreign World," 47–48.

35. For a careful interpretation see esp. Thomas R. Schreiner, "An Interpretation of 1 Timothy 2:9–15: A Dialogue with Scholarship," *Women in the Church*, 105–54.

36. See also Jesus' teaching on divorce in Matt. 19:4–6; cf. 1 Cor. 11:8–9.

37. For more on this topic see especially E. P. Clowney, *The Church* (CCT; Downers Grove: InterVarsity, 1995).

38. So *IvE* 18C; cf. Hunt & Edgar, *Select Papyri*, LCL, vol. 2, nos. 353 and 425.

39. See Plutarch's first-century essay, "On the *Daemonion* of Socrates."

40. For runaways, see *New Docs 8* (1998): 1–46.

41. Ambrosiaster, *Quaestiones veteris et novi testamenti*, 125.5, trans. by David Hunter in Wimbush, ed., *Ascetic Behavior*, 103.

42. Homer, *Iliad* 3.65.

43. See also 2 Tim. 4:3; Titus 1:9; 2:1.

44. For one example, see Diodorus Siculus, 1.23.8.

45. Plato's *Republic* has a long discussion of the faults of the major poets like Homer and Hesiod, beginning in sec. 377.

46. See, e.g., the essay "On Gymnastics" by Philostratus (3d cent. A.D.), trans. in Rachel Sargent Robinson, *Sources for the History of Greek Athletics* (Chicago: Ares, 1981; reprint of 1955 edition), 212–32. Other texts in Robinson's book are also of interest; see also Waldo E. Sweet, *Sport and Recreation in Ancient Greek: A Sourcebook with Translations* (New York and Oxford: Oxford Univ. Press, 1987).

47. Dieter Knibbe and Bülent Iplikçioglu, "Neue Inschriften aus Ephesos IX," *JOAIW* 55 (1984) Hauptblatt: 130. Cf. F. W. Danker, *Benefactor: Epigraphic Study of a Graeco-Roman and New Testament Semantic Field* (St. Louis: Clayton, 1982).

48. See S. M. Baugh, "'Savior of All People': 1 Tim. 4:10 in Context," *WTJ* 54 (1992): 331–40.

49. E.g., see 4:14; Acts 15:6; James 5:14.

50. Cf. Bruce W. Winter, *Seek the Welfare of the City: Christians as Benefactors and Citizens* (Carlisle and Grand Rapids: Paternoster and Eerdmans, 1994), 62–78; see also *New Docs 8* (1998): 106–16 for treatment of this passage in light of background materials and for current bibliography.

51. For recent discussion and bibliography of women's dowries and inheritance particularly illumined by documents from Hellenistic Egypt see *New Docs 6* (1992): 1–18. Note, however, that one must always be cautious about universalizing Egyptian evidence to other parts of the ancient world.

52. See Sarah B. Pomeroy, *Families in Classical and Hellenistic Greece: Representations and Realities* (Oxford: Clarendon, 1997), 6–7.

53. Pliny, *Ep.* 7.24.

54. See also Danker, *Benefactor*; *New Docs 8* (1998): 114.

55. Pliny, *Nat. Hist.* 14.9.75.

56. E.g., Dio Chrysostom, *Orations* 14–15.

57. For sources on ancient slavery see Thomas Wiedemann, *Greek & Roman Slavery*. The *New Documents* series also contains a nice collection of sources and discussions on different aspects of ancient slavery scattered throughout its volumes; e.g., *New Docs 6* (1992): 48–81.

58. The classic detailed description of this war was written by the Jewish turncoat, Josephus: *J.W.* (*Bellum Judaicum*).

59. 1 Tim. 6:11; see also 1:18; 2 Tim. 4:7.

60. See James M. Robinson, ed., *The Nag Hammadi Library in English* (New York, et al.: Harper and Row, 1977).

Sidebar and Chart Notes

A-1. 1 Tim. 1:4; 4:7; 6:20; 2 Tim. 2:16; 4:4; Titus 3:9; 1 Tim. 1:7; Titus 3:9; Titus 1:14; 1 Tim. 4:3; 2 Tim. 2:18; cf. 1 Cor. 15:12.

A-2. Pliny, *Letters* 6.31; *IvE* 234–35 et al.; cf. Acts 19:31 for Asiarch.

A-3. See my "Cult Prostitution in New Testament Ephesus: A Reappraisal," *JETS* 42/3 (September 1999): 443–60.

A-4. For a more complete picture consult my "A Foreign World."

A-5. Cf., e.g., *New Docs 3* (1983): 8.

A-6. The translation here is that of S. C. Barton and G. H. R. Horsley, given in "A Hellenistic Cult Group and the New Testament Churches," *JAC* 24 (1981): 7–41 (p. 9); see also esp. Stanley K. Stowers, "A Cult From Philadelphia: Oikos Religion or Cultic Association?" in *The Early Church in Its Context* (eds. A. Malherbe, F. Norris, and J. Thompson; Leiden, Boston, and Cologne: E. J. Brill, 1998), 287–301.

A-7. Pliny, *Ep.* 10.96; LCL.

A-8. See A. N. Sherwin-White, *The Letters of Pliny: A Historical and Social Commentary* (Oxford: Clarendon, 1966), 708.

A-9. Ovid, *Fasti* 4.186; Apuleius, *Golden Ass* 8; Juvenal, *Satires* 6; Seneca, *Ep.* 108.

A-10. Plutarch, "Oracles at Delphi," *Moralia* 403F LCL).

A-11. Josephus, *Ant.* 1.18.5.

A-12. See Vincent Wimbush, ed., *Ascetic Behavior in Greco-Roman Antiquity: A Sourcebook* (Minneapolis: Fortress, 1990); J. K. Elliott, *The Apocryphal New Testament* (Oxford: Clarendon, 1993), for early texts that promote various forms of asceticism.

A-13. See ibid., also, W. K. Lacey, *The Family in Classical Greece* (Ithaca, N.Y.: Cornell Univ. Press, 1968).

A-14. See Naum Jasny, "The Breads of Ephesus and Their Prices," *AH* 21 (1947): 190–92.

A-15. Joseph Dommers Vehling, ed., *Apicius: Cookery and Dining in Imperial Rome* (Chicago: Walter M. Hill, 1936; Dover reprint ed. 1977).

2 TIMOTHY

by S. M. Baugh

Second Timothy is the second of the "Pastoral Letters." For a general introduction on the authorship of these letters, see the comments at the beginning of 1 Timothy.

The Occasion for Second Timothy

In the introduction to 1 Timothy, I sketched out a probable scenario for the events in Paul's life and the background of the three Pastoral Letters. In that scenario, 2 Timothy comes as the last letter written by Paul. He was in Rome again, imprisoned and awaiting trial the second time (see 4:12–20). Since he had left some belongings at Troas, it seems that Paul had been arrested there or in some other city in Asia Minor before being sent on to Rome for trial. There is a hint in *1 Clement* 5.7 (ca. A.D. 95; cf. the later Muratorian Canon) that Paul actually made it to the "limit of the west," that is, to Spain, as he had

REMAINS OF
LAODICEA IN
ASIA MINOR

▶ **2 Timothy**
IMPORTANT FACTS:

- **AUTHOR:** The apostle Paul.
- **DATE:** Perhaps A.D. 66–67 (during Paul's second Roman imprisonment?).
- **VENUES:** Paul is probably in Rome writing to Timothy in Asia Minor.
- **OCCASION:**
  - To convey his last thoughts and exhortations to Timothy in the face of probable martyrdom (4:6–8).
  - To warn against certain false teachers and apostate brothers.
  - To further encourage Timothy in the conduct of his ministry.

hoped (Rom. 15:24, 28). If true, he would have been released from this second Roman imprisonment, unless he had already gone to Spain between his two Roman imprisonments. The massive turbulence caused by the Jewish revolt and the concurrent Roman coups and brief civil war right around this time makes this conceivable if not certain. Nero's assassination in June of 68 inaugurated the "year of the four emperors": Galba (June 68 to January 69); Otho (January to March 69); Vitellius (April to December 69); and finally, Vespasian (December 69 to 79).

Paul is writing in anticipation of his condemnation and execution at Rome (4:6). He writes to Timothy to alert him of his circumstances (2:9), to warn him of certain future dangers to the church and her doctrine (e.g., 4:3–4), and to ask Timothy and Mark to come to him and bring along certain items from Troas (4:9–13). Of all Paul's letters, this one is filled with poignant reflections by the apostle on his life's conclusion and the awareness that he must turn his ministry over to others.

Salutation and Letter Opening (1:1–2)

The letter opening and salutation here are much like those found in other letters of the time. The author first identifies

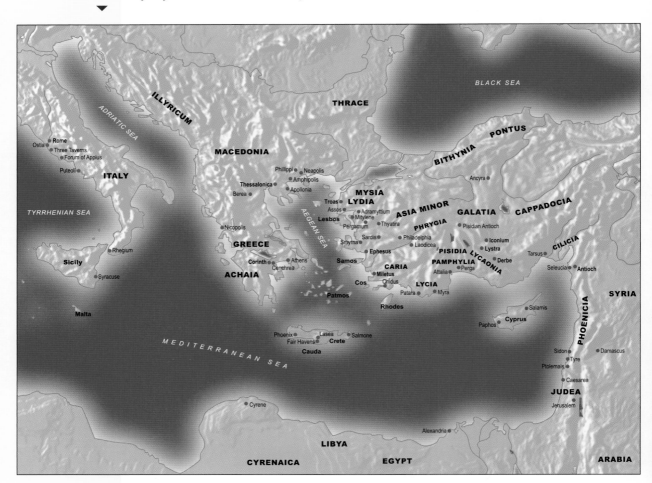

himself and then the recipient ("to Timothy, my dear son"), and he conveys his cordial respects. As often in Paul's letters, his identification includes his office, "an apostle of Christ Jesus", his divine appointment, "by the will of God", and a brief reminder of the focus of his apostolic ministry, "according to the promise of life that is in Christ Jesus." Paul is not magnifying himself, but assuring his young protégé that he is carrying on a divinely ordained ministry, even if Paul himself is soon to be martyred. Religious offices were regularly purchased in the Greek world (see accompanying box) or distributed by favor of patronage in Rome, but Paul received an appointment from God himself. This would be a striking contrast to a contemporary.

Grace, mercy and peace (1:2). Paul's greeting in 2 Timothy ends with an apostolic benediction in 1:2, "Grace, mercy and peace from God the Father and Christ Jesus our Lord." In most letters of the time, the standard opening ends with the word "greetings," or more effusive, "abundant greetings." For example, a second-century B.C. letter from Egypt begins: "Sarapion to his brothers Ptolemaeus and Apollonius *greetings*. If you are well, [it would be excellent]. I myself am well."[1] The standard word in Greek for "greetings" (*chairein*; see Acts 15:23; 23:26; James 1:1) sounds something like the Greek word for "grace" (*charis*), which suggests how the benediction came to be substituted in Christian letters.

Paul's Circumstances (1:3–18)

God, whom I serve, as my forefathers did (1:3). Paul does not usually refer to his "forefathers" as he does here. Yet he

---

▶ Sale of Religious Offices

The following letter illustrates the common practice of the sale of religious offices in the Hellenistic world as well as some of the elements of a Greek letter. This well-preserved letter happens to be an official petition, so it does not have any personal remarks. It is from an Egyptian named Pakebkis to a Roman public official. It reads:

> Copy. To Tiberius Claudius Justus, administrator of the private account, from Pakebkis son of Marsisouchus, exempted priest of the famous temple of Soknebtunis also called Cronus and the most great associated gods, which is situated in the village of Tebtunis in the division of Polemon in the Arsinoite nome. I wish to purchase the office of prophet in the aforesaid temple, which has been offered for sale for a long time, on the understanding that I shall … [missing] … and carry the palm-branches and perform the other functions of the office of prophet and receive in accordance with the orders the fifth part of all the revenue which falls to the temple, at the total price of 2200 drachmae instead of the 640 drachmae offered long ago by Marsisouchus son of Pakebkis, which sum I will pay, if my appointment is ratified, into the local public bank at the customary dates; and I and my descendants and successors shall have the permanent ownership and possession of this office forever with all the same privileges and rights, on payment (by each one) of 200 drachmae for admission. If therefore it seem good to you, my lord, you will ratify my appointment here in the city upon these terms and write to the strategus of the nome about this matter, in order that the due services of the gods who love you may be performed.[A-1]

clearly wants to bring up the issue of generational continuity in the service of God. He worships and serves God as had his Jewish ancestors. In 1:5 we see that Timothy also is continuing on in the faith of his grandmother and mother (see also 3:15). Perhaps the issue of continuity arises in Paul's mind because he knows that his life is drawing to a close, and he is therefore concerned that the next generation of ministers, like Timothy, must carry on his labors.

Continuity with one's ancestors in religion or in other areas of life was a key idea in the ancient Mediterranean world (cf. Acts 16:20–21). This is nowhere more apparent than in the noble Roman practice of making wax death masks (*imagines*) of one's parents.[2] In contrast, Paul would have no death mask made for him; however, he conveys a noble heritage of godly service at the command of the living God to Timothy, his "dear son" in the faith.[3]

In your grandmother Lois and in your mother Eunice (1:5). We have no other information about Timothy's grandmother, but of his mother we read this in Acts: "He [Paul] came to Derbe and then to Lystra, where a disciple named Timothy lived, whose mother was a Jewess

and a believer, but whose father was a Greek" (Acts 16:1). Lystra was in the district of Lycaonia in the lower regions of the rough Galatian area in Asia Minor. It is notable that Lois had married a Greek. While this violated Old Testament law, it is not the only instance of the intermarriage of Jews with Greeks in Asia Minor. For example, in Acmonia in Phyrgia, a pagan priestess named Julia Severa had donated a large synagogue to the Jewish community in the Neronian period, probably at the instigation of her second husband, a Jew named Tyronius Rapo.[4]

The physical evidence for the large Jewish settlements in Asia Minor is remarkably scanty and probably indicates a thorough assimilation and accommodation of the Jews into their surrounding cultures, where they had lived for many centuries (Isa. 60:9; Obad. 20). Note as well that both the names Lois and Eunice are Greek, not Hebrew in origin, even though Lois at least was Jewish.

Immortality (1:10). Christ brought "life and immortality to light" (1:10). By saying these words without further elaboration, Paul shows just how thoroughly Jewish is the foundation of his thought. To a Greek of his day, "immortality" was the inherent property only of the gods

and of a few heroes and benefactors who were deified. Otherwise, "mortal" was a synonym for "human being." Some in the Greco-Roman world believed in transmigration of souls or reincarnation after death since it was introduced to the Greeks by Pythagoras in the sixth century B.C. There is, for instance, a famous and vivid passage in Virgil's *Aeneid* where Aeneas visits the underworld only to see the souls of the dead as they flit across the river to reinhabit bodies in the world above (*Aeneid* 6; late first century B.C.). In contrast, the Judeo-Christian worldview is expressed in Hebrews 9:27: "Man is destined to die once, and after that to face judgment."

Of this gospel (1:11). Paul was a herald, apostle, and teacher of the "gospel" (1:11). Christian usage has established this word with specialized meaning. Yet in Paul's day it was still used by his contemporaries to mean simply "good news" of some sort. It was used, for instance, to refer to a wedding announcement, a message about some happy event in the life of the emperor or of his family (e.g., his son passing into manhood), an imperial benefaction being granted to a city, the report of a military victory, or a message of other such glad tidings. The Greek word in 1:10 (*euangelion*) is the origin of our word "evangelist." Paul tells Timothy later in this book to fulfill his calling as an "evangelist" (4:5; cf. Acts 21:8; Eph. 4:11); that is, Timothy too was to be a messenger of the "good news" of the victory and benefactions of the King of kings, Jesus Christ, "who has destroyed death and has brought life and immortality to light through the gospel" (1:10).

I was appointed a herald (1:11). In the Greek world, a herald was more than just

a town crier. Heralds made public announcements throughout a city to the citizen body like a crier, but they also acted as official messengers to other cities, carrying messages between governments. Furthermore, they assisted at public meetings, recited prayers at public sacrifices, and acted as emcees at public banquets. Paul has adapted the role of this common public figure to describe his own role as an official messenger from Christ (cf. 1 Tim. 2:7). By adding his credentials as "an apostle and a teacher," we see that his apostolic office gave him full authority from Christ to lay the foundation of the church and to instruct her in her growth in divine grace.

Everyone in the province of Asia has deserted me (1:15). Paul's exhortations to Timothy to stand firm in his ministry (1:13–14) takes on special urgency in light of the desertion from duty of "everyone in the province of Asia," particularly a certain Phygelus and Hermogenes (1:15). (Both names are Greek, but these men are otherwise unknown to us.) Paul must mean that the Christians from

WESTERN ASIA MINOR ▼

Asia Minor who were in Rome had abandoned him at his trial (cf. 4:16). Certainly other Christians in the region, like Onesiphorus (1:16) and Timothy himself who were in Asia at the time, had not forsaken him. But the desertion of many has obviously deeply grieved Paul.

Onesiphorus ... often refreshed me (1:16). Paul contrasts the desertion of others with the faithful personal ministry of one Onesiphorus, who is also mentioned in 4:19 but nowhere else in the New Testament. "Onesiphorus" means "profit-bearer" (i.e., "profitable") in Greek and is a common name given to slaves. However, the fact that Onesiphorus has a "household" or family (1:16; 4:19) shows that he was probably a freedman, since slaves usually could not marry or have children of their own. Onesiphorus's freedman status is supported by the fact that he had the ability to travel to Rome on his own to hunt down Paul in order to minister to him. Many freedmen in the Roman empire had opportunities to acquire wealth and had the leisure to travel, so there is nothing unusual in this. In fact, some of the most powerful men in the Roman empire were the emperor's freedmen and therefore of his "household" (cf. Phil. 4:22). It is notable that in the Christian community, there is absolutely no snobbery in relation to one's slave or freedman status, as there was in the world at the time.[5]

Exhortation to Faithfulness (2:1–7)

Paul continues his exhortations and warnings on false teachers to Timothy in chapter 2. The issue of false teachers has come up already in this letter as well as frequently in 1 Timothy, which should impress us not to think of the church in the apostolic age as dwelling in an idyllic golden age without trial and testing. The early church experienced the same kind of problems that plague the church today, but we also have the same resource today as then: protection given by our faithful Savior (e.g., 2:13).

Entrust to reliable men who will also be qualified to teach others (2:2). This statement shows that Paul does not envision the pastoral or teaching ministry to be the actions of one lone man, but of a plurality of leaders in the church.

A good soldier of Christ Jesus (2:3). When Paul tells Timothy to "endure hardship with us," the young pastor must act "like a good soldier" (2:3). It is the lot of all soldiers to put up with great hardships in the course of their duties, especially in wartime (cf. 4:5). We don't know exactly when 2 Timothy was composed, but it was around the time of a foiled plot to assassinate Nero in A.D. 65, led by Seneca and a tribune of a Praetorian cohort named Subrius Flavus. When asked by Nero why he broke his oath of loyalty (Latin *sacramentum*), Flavus

---

R E F L E C T I O N S

TIMOTHY, AS AN EVANGELIST—A MESSENGER OF the good news—was also to be a teacher of the "sound teaching" conveyed to him by Paul (1:13). Indeed, he was to *guard* this teaching as a "good deposit" entrusted to him (1:14). Guards were common in antiquity as now, and they tended to be rough characters. But Timothy was not to arm himself with sword or spear; rather, he was to guard his treasure through the Holy Spirit and to proclaim and teach his message "with faith and love in Christ Jesus." Christians, and especially Christian teachers, are not to take their cue from the world's ways, but from Christ's ways.

As an athlete (2:5). The athlete shares features with the soldier: Both must endure hardship before gaining the victory (cf. 4:7). Yet here Paul invokes the fact that the athlete must compete "according to the rules" if he is to acquire the victory crown, implying that Timothy must acquire his "crown of righteousness" (4:8) by contesting according to the rules governing the servant of Christ. Many of the athletic contests in the Greek world had judges. For example, vase paintings of boxing matches often depict a judge supervising the match with a switch in his hand to enforce his rulings.

The hardworking farmer (2:6). Farming in the Western world today is performed by a small minority of the population. For example, the U. S. Census Bureau lists about 2 million full- and part-time farm operators out of a total population of over 270 million people (this figure does not list all farm laborers, just the "operators" or owners of farms); this is less than 1 percent. In antiquity, however—as well as in many parts of the world today—somewhere around 85 or 90 percent of the whole population was directly involved with growing or getting food as their primary occupation. Perhaps as little as 5 percent lived in ancient cities because a city requires surplus food production in the lands under its control to support the city-dwellers. In other words, Paul's analogy of the hardworking farmer would have been much more alive to his original readers than to many of us, because many of them were farmers or had farming experience.

The first to receive a share of the crops (2:6). At first sight, it may seem strange to say that a farmer should receive a share of

replied, "Because I detested you! I was as loyal as any of your soldiers as long as you deserved affection. I began detesting you when you murdered your mother and wife and became a charioteer, actor, and incendiary!"[6]

In addition, the year and a half from June of 68 to December of 69 was soon to witness the passing of the imperial crown from Nero to Galba to Otho to Vitellius and finally to Vespasian—all because of the loyalty or the treachery of the Roman troops under each man's command. Paul was speaking in general and theoretically about the dedication of a soldier to his commanding officer, but current events were witnessing just how important loyalty of soldiers toward their leaders could be. Timothy's self-denying service was to be to the Lord of lords and King of kings, who was first loyal to his subjects to the point of death on the cross.

◀ *left*

ROMAN SOLDIER

A man modeling the typical dress of a Roman soldier at the Colosseum in Rome.

his own crops (2:6; cf. 1 Cor. 9:7). Were they not *his* crops? The answer is that they typically were not in Paul's day, since farms were often owned by absentee landlords. Ancient farmers were often like medieval serfs, who were tied to the lands they farmed but they did not own. Typically city residents, temples, or a city itself owned most of the outlying farm lands around a city.[7] It can be estimated from the placement of boundary markers that have been uncovered that the temple of Artemis of Ephesus owned as much as 77,000 acres of rich farm lands extending up to thirty miles outside the temple's precincts (which was itself about a mile outside of Ephesus). As just one example, here is a section out of the Greek novel from the period entitled *Daphnis and Chloe*, after the principal characters. The father of Chloe (the girl) approached Lamon, the father of Daphnis (the boy) to arrange a marriage between their children (although the usual custom was for the young man's father to approach the girl's). Both men worked small farmsteads with grain, grapes, and herds. Lamon responds:

> I'd be mad not to think it a great advantage to gain the friendship of your family, now that I'm an old man and need extra hands to get the work done. Besides, Chloe's a girl who's very much sought after, pretty and fresh and excellent in every way. But being a slave I can't make my own decisions about any member of my family. My master will have to be told of it and give his consent. So look here, let's put off the wedding until the autumn, for then he'll be here, according to reports that have been reaching us from town (3.31; Penguin trans.).

This small snippet illustrates many interesting features of ancient slave life (e.g., the father cannot control his son's marriage), as well as the point at hand that a slave worked relatively independently on a small farm owned by someone else in a nearby city.

Christ and Paul's Chains (2:8–13)

This section begins with a brief statement about Jesus' resurrection and messianic identity in 2:8 ("raised from the dead, descended from David"), which summarizes Paul's gospel. This reference may have been part of a longer confession of faith such as found sketched out elsewhere in the New Testament and in the early church fathers. An example of the latter is this passage from Ignatius of Antioch in his letters to the Trallian church dated ca. A.D. 108: "Be deaf therefore when anyone speaks to you apart from Jesus Christ, who was of the family of David, and of Mary, who was truly born, both ate and drank, was truly persecuted under Pontius Pilate, was truly crucified and died in the sight of those in heaven and on earth and under the earth; who also was truly raised from the dead, when his Father raised him up."[8]

Chained like a criminal (2:9). Paul refers here to his own chains. He was in prison for the sake of Christ, the gospel, and the elect (2:10). From later statements (4:6, 16), Paul was obviously awaiting trial in Rome, probably before a Roman official of the Praetorian Guard.[9] Paul had evidently been arrested and sent to Rome from either Troas or from another city in Asia Minor (4:12, 20) rather than from Jerusalem and Caesarea, as in the book of Acts. He was thus awaiting trial after undergoing a preliminary examination by the Roman magistrate (4:16–19). Paul was in chains "like a criminal" (2:9). Not all prisoners were chained, and it shows in Paul's case that the Romans thought him to be dangerous or unreliable. Paul may have been held in a private home under guard or in one of the public prisons in Rome. The Romans and Greeks did not use prison as a form of punishment, but merely as a way to detain prisoners until trial. Afterward, various punishments such as fines, confiscation of property, banishment, enslavement, hard labor in the mines, or the death sentence were meted out. Paul expected the latter (4:6).

Here is a trustworthy saying (2:11). The lines of 2:11b–13 undoubtedly comprise the "trustworthy saying" (see comments on 1 Tim. 1:15).

Instructions to Timothy (2:14–26)

A workman who does not need to be ashamed (2:15). Paul exhorts Timothy to consider his task as a Christian minister and teacher as if he were a construction engineer "who correctly handles the word of truth" (2:15; cf. *1 Clement* 34.1). Paul uses a rare verb here for "correctly handles." The etymology comes from two words meaning "to cut something straight," and the verb is found with that meaning in the Greek translation of the OT referring to the setting out of a path or roadway in a straight direction (Prov. 3:6; 11:5). If the analogy Paul invokes refers to highway engineering and since the Roman roads back then—many of which are still in use today—are marvelous examples of careful and skillful work, we can understand that Timothy was to skillfully teach the word of God in an upright manner without deviating from the straight pathway into "quarreling about words" or "godless chatter" (2:14, 16).

Their teaching will spread like gangrene (2:17). In contrast with Timothy's "sound" (or "healthy") teaching (cf. 1 Tim. 1:10; 2 Tim. 1:13), the teaching of the ungodly "will spread like gangrene"

◄

ROMAN COLOSSEUM

The photo shows the area beneath the stadium floor.

(2 Tim. 2:17). In a world where antiseptics and sterilization were unknown, gangrene was a common malady. This was particularly so in antiquity where a medical consultant was as likely as anything to have his patient visit a hot springs, sleep in the temple of the god of healing (Asclepius), or pronounce a charm over an infection. Gangrene was often the result of such treatments.

Among them are Hymenaeus and Philetus (2:17). Paul names Hymenaeus and Philetus as two of the aberrant teachers of whom Timothy is to beware. Paul has already mentioned Hymenaeus, whom he had excommunicated (see 1 Tim. 1:20), but Philetus is otherwise unknown. However, he does mention their error: They claim that the general resurrection of the dead has already occurred and thereby are destroying the faith of some (2 Tim. 2:18; cf. 1 Cor. 15). It is interesting to note that this particular heresy is making a comeback today by those who teach that the return of Christ and the general resurrection of the dead was fulfilled in A.D. 70.

Sealed with this inscription (2:19). The church of God is built on a solid foundation by God himself, who has inscribed his seal on it.[10] A seal was used in antiquity to prove the authenticity of something; in this case, God has inscribed his assurance to us that he knows his own and is secretly preserving them as well as issuing his command that all members of the visible church ("everyone who confesses the name of the Lord") must produce the good fruit of faith and turn away from evil. Inscriptions were found on all the solid marble and granite public buildings in antiquity, and the texts of these inscriptions comprise a major source for our understanding of life back then. Paul turns the commonplace sight of building inscriptions into a spiritual lesson.

Articles not only of gold and silver, but also of wood and clay (2:20). Paul refers to various kinds of "articles" or "vessels" found in a large household. Modern archaeologists have unearthed countless quantities of these objects—from delicate glass perfume jars to huge stone wine containers. The "ignoble" articles of 2:20 would include the rough clay chamber pots found in every household. There were public toilets in most of the larger cities—some with underground canals to carry away the waste—but chamber pots were still needed. The "noble" articles would include the fine table service dishes and ornamental painted ceramic jars. One common

REFLECTIONS

WHAT PAUL SAYS IN 2:18 AND OUR own observations today may discourage us about the debilitating effects of heresy on the church. But Paul does not stop with the negative. He encourages us in 2:19 by pointing to God's power and protection of the church. She is built on a solid foundation—Jesus Christ and his truth—by God himself, who has inscribed his seal on it. God owns and protects his church from all attacks external and internal, so that we can confidently sing the great hymn: "By schisms rent asunder, by heresies distressed. . . . The church shall never perish! Her dear Lord to defend, to guide, sustain, and cherish, is with her to the end" ("The Church's One Foundation," by Samuel S. Wesley).

example of the latter that every Greek household contained was a special, beautifully painted amphora given to a bride at her wedding and then displayed prominently in the home thereafter.

Escape from the trap of the devil (2:26). Paul concludes his exhortations to Timothy in this chapter by telling him to "flee the evil desires of youth" and "foolish and stupid arguments" (2:22–23). Instead, he is to gently persuade and instruct his opponents, "in the hope that God will grant them repentance leading them to a knowledge of the truth" (2:25), and thus they will escape the "trap of the devil" (2:26). Trapping was a common form of hunting in antiquity. In early days, wild boar, lions, hare, and deer were trapped with nets, sometimes with the help of hounds. Birds too were trapped in nets or by applying sticky birdlime to branches where they congregated. This is a vivid image for the deadly effects of sin.

Warning of Last Days (3:1–9)

Throughout chapter 3, Paul warns Timothy about certain trends he will encounter in the last days. The New Testament writers were unanimously convinced that we live in the "last days," the "last times," the "last hour," and even "the end of the ages."[11] One of the features of the era between the first and second advents of Christ is the presence of great wickedness (2 Tim. 3:1–5) alongside the advance of the kingdom of Christ, who must rule in the midst of his enemies (Ps. 110:2). See also this statement in Jude: "In the last times there will be scoffers who will follow their own ungodly desires."[12]

The early church fathers understood the apostolic teaching on the last days and

repeated it. For instance, Ignatius of Antioch (about A.D. 108) writes: "These are the last times. Therefore let us be modest, let us fear the long-suffering of God"; note also, "For in the last days the false prophets and the corrupters shall be multiplied."[13] The Qumran group in the desert of Judea had similar notions in some of their writings, though for them, the "final days" (1Q28a) were marked by physical warfare between the "sons of darkness" and the army of the "sons of light," that is, the sectarian group themselves (e.g., The War Scroll [1QM]), for they were "the last generation" (CD 1.12).[14] The Qumran group—whom one scholar called "fanatical separatists"—was eradicated by the Romans in about A.D. 68.

Having a form of godliness but denying its power (3:5). Today people outside of the Christian church usually do not put on a show of being *religious* and thereby adopt a "form of godliness" or "of piety." In our day, public demonstrations of piety are rare, but in antiquity, *everyone* (the Cynics and a very few others excepted) attended public religious functions. And piety in Greco-Roman religions was often measured by the size of one's donation to the public cults, so that honorific inscriptions from temple buildings often praised the person's "piety and generosity," which can be thought of together as "pious generosity." In other words, piety was commonly measured by external actions rather than by one's character. Hence, Paul says that false teachers may have the form of godliness, but the life-transforming power of true godliness begins with the fear of the Lord (Prov. 9:10) expressed as faith in Christ.

The kind who worm their way into homes (3:6). The typical large Greek home had a clear demarcation between the public areas of the house and the women's quarters (often on a second story). It was possible in a large household for a man to insinuate himself as a permanent guest under the patronage of the mistress of the house as a teacher or as a tutor for the children. Paul does not condemn the practice per se, but the morally corrupt hidden motives and practices that could result.

Just as Jannes and Jambres opposed Moses (3:8). These two names were assigned in Jewish sources to the Egyptian sorcerers who counterfeited the miracles of Moses in order to deceive Pharaoh (Ex. 7:11–22). While the names do not appear in the Old Testament text, Paul refers to them as commonly accepted figures with which many people were acquainted. For instance, we read this in the "Damascus Document" from Qumran: "For in ancient times there arose Moses and Aaron, by the hand of the prince of lights and Belial, with his cunning, raised up Jannes and his brother during the first deliverance of Israel" (CD 5.17–19). Even Pliny the Elder mentions Moses and Jannes in the same breath as well-known magicians from an earlier day.[15]

Paul's Example (3:10–17)

Persecutions, sufferings . . . in Antioch, Iconium and Lystra (3:11). The Antioch mentioned here is not the one in Syria, but the Pisidian Antioch in central Asia Minor. Pisidian Antioch was founded a few centuries earlier under the Seleucid kings and had grown in importance under Augustus. The nearby Pamphylian cities, Iconium and Lystra, were on the inland route east of Antioch, with Lystra being the hometown of Timothy. For the whole episode of persecution and Paul's experiences in these cities see Acts 13:14–

14:23. In Lystra, Paul had been stoned by some Jews who had come from Antioch and Iconium and was left for dead (Acts 14:19), so it was a vivid memory to which he alludes in 2 Timothy 3:11.

From infancy you have known the holy Scriptures (3:15). Paul refers to Timothy's knowledge of the Scriptures "from infancy." This is remarkable testimony about the widespread access to the Old Testament in Asia Minor in this period. However, it is probable that Timothy's family did not own a whole Hebrew or Greek Old Testament. There were strict regulations for copying the Hebrew Old Testament (the "Torah"). A synagogue would usually have a special copy acquired at high expense. The standard Greek translation of the Old Testament of the day was the Septuagint (abbreviated LXX), which was presumably the version read and used outside of Palestine. Therefore, Timothy would probably have learned the Scriptures through public readings of the LXX in a synagogue in Lystra, for, as we read elsewhere: "Moses has been preached in every city from the earliest times and is read in the synagogues on every Sabbath" (Acts 15:21). Public reading was common in antiquity, where books were more expensive and rarer than today (cf. Col. 4:16; Rev. 1:3; see comments on 2 Tim. 4:13 for more on ancient books). There is a possibility that Timothy attended a private Torah school, though the student would normally have had to travel to a school in Jerusalem or Judea for this instruction (cf. Acts 22:3).

All Scripture is God-breathed (3:16). Second Timothy 3:16–17 have been foundational for our understanding of the nature of the divine inspiration of Scripture, especially the word rendered "God-breathed" (Gk. *theopneustos*). This word itself is rare, though not without analogies in the Greek language—for example, in Homer, the god Apollo "in-breathes" strength into Aeneas during battle with words of encouragement.[16] Compound words with "God" (or the names of various Greek deities) are common in Greek as adjectives and personal names (e.g., *theodidaktos*, meaning "God-taught"; the name Theophilus, meaning "God's friend" [cf. Luke 1:3; Acts 1:1]).

Book 5 of the *Sibylline Oracles* is probably the work of an Egyptian Jew (and others) between about A.D. 90 and 130. The word *theopneustos* appears in the *Oracles* to refer to man as "God-breathed" with the breath of life at creation (*Sib. Or.* 5.406; cf. Gen. 2:7). Paul clearly means something more special, however, since it is the *Scriptures* into which God pours his breath as one who speaks through them (cf. esp. Gal. 3:8, 22; 2 Peter 1:21). They are the very words of God.[17]

The religions of Greece and Rome in Paul's time were not dependent on written materials. There were sacred books containing oracular materials (e.g., the *Sibylline Oracles*), magic books with spells, incantations, charms, and so forth (cf. Acts 19:19), and other kinds of handbooks on practices such as augury (the interpretation of various omens). Moreover, the writing of the ancient poets like Homer or Hesiod were regarded as having particular authority in their myths about the gods, though at the same time there was a popular saying: "The poets tell many lies," especially about the gods.[18] In contrast, both Judaism and its offspring, Christianity, were and are religions that rely heavily on the inspired and authoritative Scriptures.

Charge to Faithful Service (4:1–5)

Paul gives Timothy a most solemn charge to carry out his full ministry of the Word based on the certain return of Christ, his kingdom, and the certain knowledge of opposition even within the church. Once again we see that the early church was threatened by serious apostasy and schismatic teaching, which Paul says will satisfy only the cravings of those who reject "sound teaching" in place of "myths" (4:3–4; cf. comments on 1 Tim. 4:6–7).

Do the work of an evangelist (4:5). Timothy is charged to be an "evangelist" or announcer of the glad tidings (see comments on 1:11). The term "evangelist" occurs only two other times in the New Testament: Ephesians 4:11, where it appears in a list of officers along with apostles, prophets, and pastors and teachers; and in Acts 21:8, where it describes Philip (see, e.g., 8:12, 40). There is no sense here that Timothy held a separate office from other pastors and teachers of the "presbytery" (1 Tim. 4:14). But Paul is charging him to focus on the Word of God in his ministry: "preach the Word . . . correct, rebuke and encourage. . . . Do the work of an evangelist" (2 Tim. 4:2, 5).

Paul's Final Reflections (4:6–18)

Poured out like a drink offering (4:6). Paul's "being poured out like a drink offering" is a metaphor of his coming departure from this life. Drink offerings or libations of wine were poured out as part of the Old Testament sacrificial service (Num. 4:7), but they were also a common part of Greek and Roman cult practice as an accompaniment of prayer. The farmer might pour a libation at the start of each day, though the early Greek poet Hesiod gives this warning: "Never pour a libation of sparkling wine to Zeus after dawn with unwashed hands, nor to others of the deathless gods; else they do not hear your prayers but spit them back."[19] When embarking on a sea voyage, sailors would pour a bowl of wine into the sea with prayers for safety; on making landfall on foreign soil, Jason and the Argonauts poured a libation of honeyed wine on the earth to ask the gods and heroes of the place for a kind welcome.[20]

At other times, such as before a battle or another great venture, a special libation was poured out to accompany prayers for a successful outcome.[21] Libations also topped off a sacrifice, with the worshiper pouring wine or some other liquid on the altar after the burnt offering was mostly consumed. Finally, libations were also a standard part of any occasion where wine was drunk as a token of thanks to the gods. In Paul's case, he says that his life itself is a sacrificial prayer about to be poured out to the true God (cf. Phil. 2:17).

The crown of righteousness (4:8). There is no more common picture in the ancient Greek world of a successful athlete who was awarded a crown as his prize. For instance, a victor at the Olympic games

REFLECTIONS

PAUL, IN CONTRAST WITH THE PER- ishable military and athletic crowns of his day, was looking forward to receiving an imperishable "crown of righteousness." This crown is a free gift offered to all who have longed for the appearance of "the righteous Judge" (4:8).

was given a wreath of olive branches. But military victors were also given a crown. Pliny the Elder mentions several of the Roman military crown awards while discussing the *corona graminea,* "crown of grass"—also called the *corona obsidionalis,* "siege-crown"—as follows:

> No crown indeed has been a higher honour than the crown of grass among the rewards for glorious deeds given by the sovereign people, lords of the earth. Jewelled crowns, golden crowns, crowns for scaling enemy ramparts or walls, or for boarding men-of-war, the civic crown for saving the life of a citizen, the triumph crown—these were instituted later than this grass crown, and all differ from it greatly, in distinction as in character. . . . This same crown is called the siege crown when a whole camp has been relieved and saved from awful destruction.[22]

The Roman grass crown was, as its name suggests, a wreath plaited from ordinary grass, yet it was prized above all other military decorations. Pliny could find mention of only eight recipients over the span of several centuries.[23]

Demas . . . has deserted me (4:10). Paul names various people in 4:9–14: Demas (familiar form of Demetrius) was Paul's "fellow worker" (Philem. 24; cf. Col. 4:14), yet here he has abandoned Paul for Thessalonica, perhaps his hometown; Crescens (a Roman name) and Titus departed for other places, perhaps at Paul's request (cf. Titus 3:12). Luke is presumably the "beloved physician" (Col. 4:14, NRSV; cf. Philem. 24), who alone stayed with Paul in his hour of need. Mark is obviously John Mark, who had left prematurely during Paul's first mis-

sionary journey (Acts 12:25; 13:5, 13). It appears that Paul's former breach with Mark was now healed (Philem. 24; cf. 1 Peter 5:13). Tychicus was Paul's messenger for other letters and a fellow worker (Acts 20:4; Eph. 6:21; Col. 4:7). Carpus (Gk. word meaning "fruitful") and Alexander the metalworker are mentioned only here in the New Testament. Troas was a coastal city in northwest Asia Minor and was a natural point of departure for ships sailing for Rome.

When you come, bring the cloak (4:13). Paul asks Timothy to bring along a cloak he had left behind at Troas with a man named Carpus. This garment was a heavy tunic or overcoat worn over the normal outer garment in the cold winter months. The material was normally of a thick wool and was fairly valuable. Paul is evidently writing in late summer and wants Timothy to get his winter overcoat to him before the cold sets in (cf. 4:21).

And my scrolls (4:13). We know from ancient sources as well as from rich remains of papyrus documents that have survived in the dry sands of Egypt that the "scrolls" or "books" to which Paul refers were papyrus rolls, used for all kinds of writings. Papyrus was manufactured exclusively in Egypt in this period and jealously regulated by the Roman authorities, especially after a shortage of papyrus under Tiberius had caused alarm among the imperial bureaucrats.[24] The standard size scroll was sold in twenty sheet lengths. Longer works would require the copyist to glue more sheets onto the roll, though this could make the work unwieldy. Each sheet was four to nine inches wide, so that a standard scroll was roughly seven to fifteen feet long. Imagine trying to find a favorite passage at the end of a 15 foot

▶ The Library at Ephesus

One of the most notable features of the archaeological remains of ancient Ephesus is the Celsus library (built from A.D. 110 to 135). This beautiful edifice could house thousands of scrolls and books and was in a central part of town, where public lectures were conducted, perhaps even the vicinity of "the lecture hall of Tyrannus," where Paul had taught (Acts 19:9). Libraries and bookseller stalls were a common feature of big cities in antiquity and show that books were easily obtainable in antiquity.

long papyrus scroll. This problem encountered by early Christians trying to look things up in the New Testament documents is thought to have contributed to the rising popularity of the "codex" style of book, which we know today.[25]

What did Paul's scrolls contain? Copies of his own works? We do know that ancient authors—as do modern ones—normally kept copies of their works on hand. Or did Paul own a copy of the Gospel of John perhaps, with which his expressions show some remarkable similarity? Or were these Septuagint scrolls of the Old Testament? There is no way of knowing, of course, but it is tempting to speculate.

Especially the parchments (4:13). The word Paul uses for "parchments" is a Latin word (*membrana*) brought into Greek. Parchment was made from sheepskin or goatskin and provided a durable writing surface. Parchment required a special ink to adhere to it and it could be more expensive than papyrus, although it also allowed the advantage of being somewhat erasable when the ink from a previous work was scraped off the surface, producing a *palimpsest* or "redone" manuscript. If much erasing was anticipated, wax tablets were used, especially for school workbooks.

Some scholars believe that the word for "especially" in 4:13 is mistranslated. They prefer to read the Greek word as communicating clarifying information: "bring . . . my scrolls, *that is*, the parchments."[26] However, I am persuaded that "especially" in our versions is correct after examining all the New Testament and other ancient evidence adduced to support this rendering.

At my first defense (4:16). We cannot know the precise details of Paul's trial(s) in Rome; however, we know generally how such trials were conducted and we have the account of Paul's examinations in Judea under Felix and Festus in Acts 23–

right ▶

ORATOR

Statue of Demosthenes (384–322 B.C.), the greatest Athenian orator.

25.[27] Paul mentions that he had been given a first defense, at which he undoubtedly took the occasion to preach Christ (2 Tim. 4:17) as he had in the defenses recorded in Acts (e.g., Acts 26). We do not know if Nero himself heard Paul's first defense or whether it was someone else. Early in his career, Nero left the mundane judicial and administrative details of his empire to his high advisors, including the popular Stoic teacher, Seneca.

I was delivered from the lion's mouth (4:17). Condemned criminals and many of the early Christian martyrs were often literally killed by lions or other beasts in the Roman amphitheaters. In this case, though, Paul is probably speaking metaphorically, since as a Roman citizen—even one from the provinces—he would not normally have been subjected to the amphitheater. Decapitation was the normal form of execution for a Roman citizen. Normally, only condemned slaves or *peregrini* (i.e., non-Roman inhabitants of the empire) died in the animal *venationes*, "hunts," testimony to the brutality possible under Roman rule.

Final Greetings (4:19–23)

Get here before winter (4:21). Paul wants Timothy to come to him before winter partly because he wants his winter overcoat (see comments on 4:13) and partly because winter travel at sea on small sailing ships was a dicey thing in antiquity (cf. Acts 27:9). The ships of the day were square-rigged, which made for slow sailing if the wind was on either beam (see accompanying box). It is

▶ Ships and Shipping

Ships of the period were constructed from edge-joined planks uniquely joined together, caulked with pitch, strengthened with interior frames, and finished off with an outer covering of lead sheathing. During storms, stout ropes were passed underneath the hull to strengthen it (Acts 27:17). The largest of the merchant ships could reach 180 feet long and 45 feet in beam, though most were smaller, some as small as a rowboat for local transport and fishing. The square sails on the larger ships allowed a typical speed of about four knots with the wind behind or on an aft quarter; however, if the wind came from a slight forward quarter the best they could do was to tack in a zigzag pattern or to wait for a change of wind direction. Some merchant galleys had oars manned by as many as 50 sailors during periods of calm or contrary winds. One or two large oars rigged to the aft sides of the ship acted as rudders when twisted on a pivot.

Pompey the Great had uprooted pirates from the eastern Mediterranean in a famous campaign in the previous century, so merchant ships in Paul's day plied the sea in relative safety and freedom and carried passengers on a space-available basis (Acts 21:2–3). Cargo holds were typically filled with grain, wine, or oil, as well as pottery, building stone, luxury items, and a wide variety of other goods (cf. Rev. 18:11–13), usually held in large earthenware jars. Investment in ships, cargoes, or single cruises was an important speculative financial opportunity in antiquity, sometimes yielding huge profits (cf. 18:17–18), or ending with disaster if the ship was wrecked.[A-2] Smaller vessels called "coasters" skimmed along the Mediterranean coastlines, trading from town to town along the way (Acts 21:1). Longer trips by bigger ships were made from the great seaports like Ephesus, Alexandria (cf. 27:6; 28:11), the Phoenician ports of Sidon and Tyre, and Puteoli near Naples (28:13).

estimated that these vessels could probably make an average speed of four or five knots over the course of a voyage, though much depended on the season, the winds, and the skill of the sailors.

Greet Priscilla and Aquila . . . (4:19). Paul ends this letter to Timothy with greetings to and from various people, which typify ancient letters, and with a report on the whereabouts of other colleagues (i.e., Priscilla, Aquila, Onesiphorus, Erastus, Trophimus, Eubulus, Pudens, Linus, and Claudia). Some of these people are known from elsewhere in the New Testament and some not, but we can see that Paul has not been entirely abandoned. The letter ends with the apostolic benediction: "The Lord be with your spirit. Grace be with you" (4:22).

ANNOTATED BIBLIOGRAPHY

Dibelius, Martin, and Hans Conzelmann. *The Pastoral Epistles*. Hermeneia. Philadelphia: Fortress, 1972.

This critical commentary relies on the typical reasons for rejecting Pauline authorship of the Pastorals, but helpfully gives detailed attention to the historical background and especially connections of the Pastoral Letters with the Hellenistic world.

Fee, Gordon D. *1 and 2 Timothy, Titus*. GNC. San Francisco: Harper & Row, 1984.

This is a concise commentary by a well-regarded NT and text-critical scholar in a popular format.

Guthrie, Donald. *The Pastoral Epistles: An Introduction and Commentary*. TNTC. Leicester and Grand Rapids: InterVarsity and Eerdmans, 1990 (rev. ed.).

A solid though brief commentary by a senior evangelical NT scholar.

Kelly, J. N. D. *A Commentary on the Pastoral Epistles*. TC. London: A. & C. Black, 1963; reprinted Grand Rapids: Baker, 1981.

This brief commentary sticks closely to the text and is marked by Kelly's characteristic sound judgment. Kelly is well versed in original sources and has produced a number of standard works in the later development of early Christianity, which add depth to his commentary.

Kidd, Reggie M. *Wealth and Beneficence in the Pastoral Epistles: A "Bourgeois" Form of Early Christianity?* Atlanta: Scholars, 1990.

This is the best of many such studies on the contemporary social and ethical background of the Pastoral Letters. Kidd surveys an extensive range of background material in this work.

Knight, George W. III. *Commentary on the Pastoral Epistles*. NIGTC. Grand Rapids and Carlisle: Eerdmans and Paternoster, 1992.

This detailed commentary on the Greek text of the Pastorals often gives illuminating historical insights as well as careful attention to the meaning of the grammar and language of the biblical text. The best technical commentary on the Pastorals in print today.

Lau, Andrew L. *Manifest in Flesh: The Epiphany Christology of the Pastoral Epistles*. WUNT 2/86. Tübingen: J. C. B. Mohr (Paul Siebeck), 1996.

This specialized study draws especially helpful connections between the epiphany material in the Pastorals with the OT and other Jewish literature.

Oden, Thomas C. *First and Second Timothy and Titus*. Interpretation. Louisville: John Knox, 1989.

Oden presents an elegant and sane defense of Pauline authorship in this topically arranged "commentary." There are a few rough spots regarding historical background of the biblical world (e.g., sacred prostitution at Ephesus, p. 95), but Oden augments his own helpful insights with a sprinkling of quotations of church fathers and Reformers, which gives the reader a wider view of the interpretation of the Pastoral Letters.

Young, Frances. *The Theology of the Pastoral Letters*. NTT. Cambridge: Cambridge Univ. Press, 1994.

This volume in a promising series spends considerable time trying to establish pseudonymous authorship of the Pastorals. Nevertheless, Young usefully reports on historical backgrounds of the Pastorals in places—for instance, on "teaching and learning in the ancient world" (pp. 79–84), though it seems mostly secondary and derivative.

Main Text Notes

1. P.Par. 43; LCL trans., emphasis added.
2. See Polybius 6.53.
3. Cf. 1 Cor. 4:17; Phil. 2:22.
4. See S. Applebaum, "The Legal Status of the Jewish Communities in the Diaspora," in *The Jewish People in the First Century* (eds. S. Safrai and M. Stern; Philadelphia: Fortress, 1976), 1.443.
5. For instance, there are several barbs hurled at imperial freedmen scattered throughout Juvenal's *Satires*.
6. Tacitus, *Ann.* 15:67; Penguin trans.
7. See *IvE* 3501–12; Dieter Knibbe et al., "Der Grundbesitz der ephesischen Artemis im Kaystrolstal," *ZPE* 33 (1979): 139–46.
8. Ignatius, *Trallians* 9.1–2.
9. See Acts 28:16 and discussion in A. N. Sherwin-White, *Roman Society and Roman Law in the New Testament* (Oxford: Oxford Univ. Press, 1963), 108–12; cf. Tajra, *Trial of St. Paul*.
10. Cf. Matt. 16:18; 1 Cor. 3:10–12; Eph. 2:20.
11. 2 Tim. 3:1; cf. Acts 2:17; Heb. 1:2; James 5:3; cf. Isa. 2:2; Hos. 3:5; 1 Peter 1:20; 1 John 2:18; Heb. 9:26.
12. Jude 18; cf. 2 Peter 3:3; 1 John 2:18.
13. Ignatius, *Ephesians* 11.1; *Didache* 16.3.
14. The Qumran materials can be found in: Florentino García Martínez, *The Dead Sea Scrolls Translated*, 2d ed. (New York, Cologne, and Grand Rapids: E. J. Brill and Eerdmans, 1996).
15. Pliny, *Nat. Hist.* 30.11.
16. Homer, *Iliad* 20.110.
17. The seminal work on Scripture and on the word *theopneustos* in 2 Tim. 3:16 is that of the old Princeton scholar, B. B. Warfield: *The Inspiration and Authority of the Bible* (Oxford: Oxford Univ. Press, 1927; repr. 1948 by Presbyterian and Reformed), esp. chap. 6.
18. E.g., Dio Chrysostom, *Or.* 18.3; Plato, *Republic* 376E–378E; Plutarch, *Moralia* 16A.
19. Hesiod, *Works and Days* 724–26.
20. Thucydides 6.32.1–2; *Argonautica* 2.1271–75.
21. E.g., *Iliad* 9.175f.; 16.225ff.
22. Pliny, *Nat. Hist.* 22.4.
23. Ibid., 22.5–7.
24. See Pliny (*Nat. Hist.*13.68–89) for this crisis and for his survey of the papyrus manufacturing process.
25. See C. H. Roberts and T. C. Skeat, *The Birth of the Codex* (Oxford: Clarendon, 1983); Naphtali Lewis, *Papyrus in Classical Antiquity* (Oxford: Clarendon, 1974).
26. T. C. Skeat, "'Especially the Parchments': A Note on 2 Timothy IV.13," *JTS* 30 (1979): 173–77.
27. The principal works on this subject are: Tajra, *Trial of St. Paul*; Brian Rapske, *Paul in Roman Custody* (Grand Rapids: Eerdmans, 1994); though A. N. Sherwin-White's *Roman Society and Roman Law* is still very useful.

Sidebar and Chart Notes

A-1. P.Tebt. 294; LCL trans..
A-2. Cf. Shakespeare, *The Merchant of Venice*.

TITUS

by S. M. Baugh

The Occasion for Paul's Letter to Titus

I have already addressed briefly the issues of Pauline authorship and the probable background scenario for the composition of Titus (see the introduction to 1 Timothy). The letter to Titus was probably written between the time of Paul's first trial in Rome as narrated in Acts and a second Roman trial that forms the background to the writing of 2 Timothy. Paul's witness in Crete while on his way to Rome the first time (Acts 27) had formed an embryonic church, which he would naturally have wished to firmly establish upon his release. He had left Titus in Crete to carry on the work (Titus 1:5) while he himself set off for Nicopolis in western Greece. It was after this second, longer stay in Crete that Paul wrote the letter to Titus. Whether Paul wrote it from Nicopolis or while on his way there (or whether he arrived there at all) is unknown. But the main concerns of Paul in this letter show his concern that Titus be further equipped

CRETE

The harbor at Fair Havens.
◄

▶ **Titus**
IMPORTANT FACTS:

- **AUTHOR:** The apostle Paul.
- **DATE:** ca. A.D. 66 (just before Paul's second Roman imprisonment?).
- **VENUES:** Paul on his way to or in Nicopolis in Epirus (western Greece), writing to Titus on the island of Crete.
- **OCCASION:**
  - To give Titus specific and general instructions for his ministry in Crete.
  - To remind Titus of Christian doctrines and ethical teachings.
  - To warn against false teachers and apostate brothers.

for his ministry to the church on Crete and to give him various other personal instructions.

Paul intends to send either Artemas (otherwise unknown) or Tychicus to take over the work in Crete so that Titus can come to join him in Nicopolis before winter sets in.[1] As mentioned, Paul is either already in Nicopolis or about to go there.

There were several places named Nicopolis in the Greek world. The word means "Victory City" and was the name of cities founded by Alexander, Pompey, and Augustus to celebrate their military successes. This Nicopolis is the one on the western coast of Greece in the province of Epirus (about 200 miles west and slightly north of Athens), founded by Augustus in 31–29 B.C. to celebrate his victory over Mark Antony. It was a Roman colony—meaning that it was originally a source of land grants for Augustus's veterans on their discharge. This city served as the regional economic and administrative capitol of the province of Epirus. Paul would naturally have gone there if he were going to Rome or returning from there.

Salutation and Letter Opening (1:1–4)

As often in Paul's letters, this letter's opening has a host of theological points to consider. It is as if Paul cannot wait to

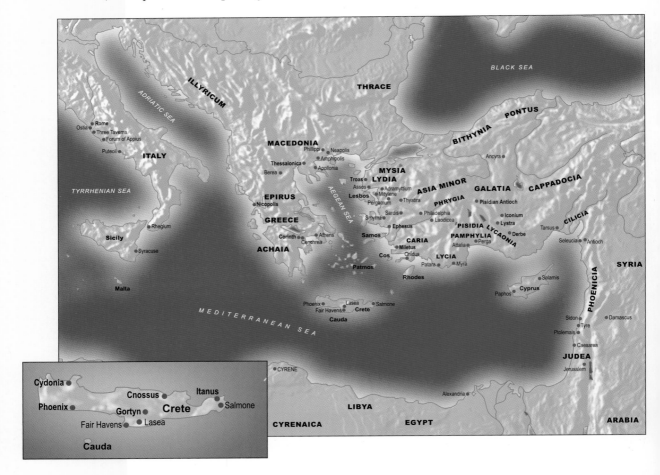

get to the body of the letter to glory in the gospel of Christ. Paul stresses his particular appointment to be an apostle—not to boast over against Titus, but, as in 1 Timothy 2:4–7, to show conclusively that God has by his appointment testified to his plan that even Gentiles (like Titus and the Cretans) are to be included in the covenant people of God (see comments on 1 Tim. 2:4–7).

God, who does not lie (1:2). When Paul says that God does not lie (1:2; cf. Heb. 6:18) and that he has promised eternal life to all who believe, Paul is speaking in light of two lying groups: (1) the Cretans, among whom Titus is working and who "are always liars" (Titus 1:12); and (2) the Greek/Cretan gods, who were ever lying and deceiving in the classical myths. There was never a greater lying trickster than Olympian Zeus, who always seemed to wrap himself in a fog in order to ravish some maiden out of sight from his wife, Hera, and then to lie about the deed. This caused some of the pagans embarrassment, which early Christian apologists exploited.[2]

To Titus, my true son (1:4). Titus, despite his Roman name, was a Greek who was an early companion of Paul in his missionary ventures (Gal. 2:1, 3). He is not mentioned in Acts, but Paul elsewhere speaks of him in the highest collegial terms (e.g., 2 Cor. 8:23). In addition to his work with Paul, Titus was now working on his own in Crete and would later go to Dalmatia (2 Tim. 4:10). He was called the first bishop of Crete in church tradition.

Titus's Task on Crete (1:5–16)

Husband of but one wife (1:6). When Paul tells Titus in 1:6 that the elder is to be the "husband of but one wife," he says something clear enough at first glance: Men who have more than one wife are excluded (cf. 1 Tim. 3:2, 12; also "wife of one husband" in 5:9). However, we run into a problem here because Greeks and Romans of the time did not practice polygamy; they were unambiguously monogamous. In consequence, we are left with only two options for understanding this statement about "husband of but one wife."

(1) The first option is that the man or wife involved must not be divorced and remarried. Divorce for the Greeks and Romans was fairly common, especially among the upper classes. Divorce could be initiated by either party (or even by the wife's father) and was usually the result of some failure to provide the basic requirements of the implicit contract, for instance, house and board or legitimate children. Read, for example, this statement in Dio Chrysostom (ca. A.D. 40–110), in a dialogue on slavery where one of his characters says: "Yes, I know that freeborn women often palm off other persons' children as their own on account of their childlessness, when they are unable to conceive children themselves, because each one wishes to keep her own husband and her home."[3] Clearly a Greek woman feared divorce for childlessness; raising up one or more heirs was considered vital to Greek and Roman families. A Greek man could also divorce his wife out of his obligation in order to marry a female heiress within his clan (an *epikleros*).[4]

(2) Paul perhaps means that a prospective elder should not have one or more concubines. This seems more likely to be Paul's meaning, for many Greeks and Romans of the time practiced concubinage. In the Greek world a Greek

man married around age thirty—in contrast, girls normally married around age fourteen—and it was taken for granted that before manhood "wild oats should be sown and done with. . . . Youth rates a certain indulgence."[5] This could occur with courtesans (*hetairai*) at the dinner parties (*symposia*) that a young man attended in a special room of Greek homes called the *andron* ("banquet hall," but more literally, "men's hall"). Furthermore, some men purchased courtesans as slaves and kept them as mistresses outside the home, while some married men had one or more concubines among the slave-girls in their households. "Don't many Athenian men have relations with their maidservants, some of them secretly, but others quite openly?"[6] Evidence for these practices is widespread.[7]

The same practices can be found among the Romans. Pliny the Younger, for example, reports on the murder of a Roman noble by a few of his slaves and mentions in a tellingly off-handed manner that the dead man's concubines raised a dreadful din on discovery of the dying man.[8] Neither the Greeks nor the

REFLECTIONS

THE LIES OF THE FALSE TEACHERS who focus on "Jewish myths" (1:14) can be discerned by their lives: They are given over to all kinds of corrupt practices (1:15–16). This demonstrates a fundamental biblical principle: Evil doctrine necessarily yields evil fruit. Good doctrine, on the other hand, must yield good fruit. The corollary to this is found in Psalm 119:100: "I have more understanding than the elders, for I obey your precepts."

Romans regarded these practices as adultery or polygamy. The Greeks conceived adultery as a sexual liaison of a free married woman with a man (married or not), but not of a man, married or not, with an unmarried woman.

Paul, as would any Jew, regards this common practice of concubinage the same as polygamy, since the sexual union is tantamount to a marital union (e.g., Gen. 2:24; 1 Cor. 6:16). Hence, he says that the overseer should be the "husband of but one wife," because union with a concubine or a prostitute constitutes another marital relation.

Cretans are always liars (1:12). The church fathers attributed the quotation on the Cretans in Titus 1:12 to Epimenides of Crete, a legendary figure from the seventh to sixth century B.C., whose works have all been lost. The line given here, "Cretans are always liars," does appear in the Hellenistic poet Callimachus, but he was not from Crete and thus not the "one of their own prophets," which Paul has in mind.[9] It was commonly understood in antiquity that the Cretans were a particularly cunning and self-serving lot, even by the Greeks who themselves deified sly tricksters like Odysseus (hero of Homer's *Odyssey* and many other tales). The Greek verb *kretizō*, "to Cretonize," meant "to double deal" and "to lie" all rolled into one (see also the accompanying box).

Instructions for Various Members of the Church (2:1–10)

Titus is told how to instruct various groups within the church: older men (2:2), older women (2:3), younger women (2:4–5; instructed by older women), and younger men (2:6). Then he mentions the instruction to be given to slaves (2:9–10). The instructions here focus on Christian character. Older men are to display a character that is "worthy of respect" (2:2). Older women are to live in such a way that they can instruct younger women to be godly homemakers (2:3–5), while younger men are to be "self-controlled" (2:6). Titus himself is to live out his own Christian integrity in order to silence any calumny that Christians merely spout high morals but live corrupt lives (2:7–8).

Older men to be . . . self-controlled (2:2). One recurring quality throughout 2:1–8 is the notion of "self-control." Paul wants older men, younger women, and younger men to demonstrate "self-control" (2:2, 5–6; cf. 1:8). In addition, he

---

▸ # A Lying Cretan

The Hellenistic era historian Polybius (ca. 200–118 B.C.) records an episode that characterizes the attitude of the ancients toward Cretans. In 223/222 B.C. a royal viceroy of the Seleucid King Antiochus III named Achaeus had recovered lands for his king in Asia Minor from the Pergamene Empire, but he turned around and proclaimed himself king of these territories in 220 while Antiochus was away putting down rebels and fighting King Ptolemy of Egypt. Antiochus duly arrived on the scene and besieged Achaeus in Sardis, which was fairly impregnable.

Friends of Achaeus hatched a plot to get him out of Sardis from under Antiochus's nose and entrusted the affair to one of King Ptolemy's high officials named Bolis, who, Polybius tells us, was a Cretan and therefore "naturally astute" (8.16). Bolis arrived in Asia Minor and took counsel with his kinsman, Cambylus, who "discussed the matter from a thoroughly Cretan point of view," which meant that "they did not take into consideration either the rescue of the man in danger [Achaeus] or their loyalty to those who had charged them with the task, but only their personal security and advantage. Both of them, then, Cretans as they were, soon arrived at the same decision," which was to make off with the money given them to free Achaeus and to approach King Antiochus for more if they could turn Achaeus over to him (8.16).

Bolis, being a Cretan and therefore "ready to entertain every kind of suspicion regarding others" (8.20), came up with a cunning plan and secretly met with Achaeus to offer to smuggle him out of Sardis, while he really intended to nab Achaeus and turn him over to his enemy. Achaeus was ready to cooperate, though he introduced a few wrinkles of his own just in case there was some double-crossing. Polybius remarks: "Achaeus indeed was doing his best, but he did not consider that, as the saying is, he was trying to play the Cretan with a Cretan [lit. *kretizō*, "to Cretanize"]; for there was no probable precaution of this kind that Bolis had not minutely examined" (8.19). The sly and double-dealing Bolis succeeded and brought about the doom of Achaeus, showing just how futile it was to try "to Cretanize a Cretan."

uses a cognate verb when he says that older women, who display a high character, "can *train* the younger women" (2:4; emphasis added). There are other words for "train," "instruct," or "advise" in Greek, and the word used here is rare (occurring only here in the NT), so Paul wants us to see it as connected to the adjective "self-controlled" used in this section.

The words related to "self-control" in 2:1–6 are used often in ancient Greek and Roman discussions of ethics. The adjective form (Gk. *sōphrōn*) may also be rendered "prudent," as a quality of someone who displays thoughtful care in his or her conduct. It can also be rendered "chaste," particularly as it relates to the conduct of women; chastity and faithfulness in wives was a virtue especially prized by the ancient Greeks (and Romans). There are many examples, but the following tomb epigram will illustrate: "Praise the affection on the part of her husband, stranger, as you read of the wife of Stabulio, Cornelia Fortunata. She continued respectable, modest (*sōphrōn*), and left him sympathetic tears."[10]

To be busy at home (2:5). Interest in "family values" such as found in 2:3–5, was not rare in the first century. The emperor Augustus was so concerned about the lack of family interest among the Roman nobility (and thereby cutting off the lines of the old Roman families) that he passed a law penalizing Romans who did not marry or have legitimate children.[11] The historian Cassius Dio (born ca. A.D. 164) writes of an incident in the Forum when some Roman knights urged Augustus to repeal this law. Augustus had the unmarried and childless stand in one part of the assembly and the married and those with children stand in another. Seeing how few the latter were in number, Dio puts a long speech into Augustus's mouth about the duty of citizens to imitate the Romans of old, who were noble not only in military prowess

CRETE

The harbor at Phoenix.

but also in the size of their population, and to imitate even the gods themselves, who marry and beget children (36.2). He continues (in Dio's account):

You have done right, therefore, to imitate the gods and right to emulate your fathers, so that, just as they begot you, you also may bring others into the world; that, just as you consider them and name them ancestors, others also may regard you and address you in similar fashion; that the works which they nobly achieved and handed down to you with glory, you also may hand on to others; and that the possessions which they acquired and left to you, you also may leave to others sprung from your own loins. For is there anything better than a wife who is *chaste, domestic,* a good house-keeper, a rearer of children; one to gladden you in health, to tend you in sickness; to be your partner in good fortune, to console you in misfortune; to restrain the mad passion of youth and to temper the unseasonable harshness of old age? (36.3; LCL trans.; emphasis added).

The words rendered "chaste" and "domestic" in the original are the same as "self-controlled" and "busy at home" in Titus 2:5.

Slaves . . . not to talk back (2:9). Paul gives Titus instructions on what to teach slaves regarding their behavior toward their masters. These instructions recall those he has given elsewhere (e.g., Eph. 6:5–8; 1 Tim. 6:1–2). As mentioned in connection with 1 Timothy 6:1–2, perhaps more than one-third of the population of the cities of the time were slaves, and certainly more if you count freedmen. Paul wants slaves to act honestly

toward their masters and "not to talk back to them" (Titus 2:9). This latter instruction may seem unneeded to us, but to the ancients the insolent slave was a typical item of conversation portrayed in their literature and plays. For instance, in Menander's play *The Girl from Samos,* as is typical of many of his and of others' comic plays, the slaves are often insolent. In one scene a saucy cook and another slave appear when the second one bursts out: "For God's sake, Cook! I can't imagine why you bother to carry knives around with you. You're quite capable of slicing through everything with your tongue" (lines 282–84).[12] It is in light of this common portrayal of the insolence of slaves that Paul wants them to quietly obey their masters "so that in every way they will make the teaching about God our Savior attractive" (2:10).

The Gospel Summarized (2:11–15)

Our great God and Savior, Jesus Christ (2:13). The focus of Titus's teaching, Paul says, is to be the glorious work and future appearance of "our great God and Savior, Jesus Christ." The rendering of this latter

---

REFLECTIONS

WE SHOULD READ THE WORD "REDEEM" IN 2:13 IN light of ancient slavery. To "redeem" someone in antiquity meant to purchase their freedom either from slavery or by way of ransom from pirates or kidnappers (who often sold their victims into slavery as well). It was no dead metaphor in Paul's day to say that Jesus Christ "gave himself for us to *redeem* us from all wickedness" (2:14; emphasis added). Here slavery to sin and captivity to its deathly consequences are portrayed as the chains that only our "great God and Savior" could break by giving himself over to death in our place.

phrase in the NIV makes it appear that Paul is calling Jesus Christ both God and Savior. This causes trouble for some commentators who believe that the New Testament writers do not ascribe divinity to Christ; hence, they prefer to read "the great God" and "our Savior, Jesus Christ" as independent from one another.[13] However, the original expression is perfectly clear in Greek; Paul is unambiguously giving Jesus Christ both titles here. It is significant that the Apostolic Fathers, the immediate heirs of the apostles, had no trouble ascribing deity to Christ in unequivocal fashion. For instance, Ignatius spoke of "our God, Jesus Christ" or of "the passion of my God" or of Christ as "from eternity with the Father."[14] The church fathers were not infallible, of course, but neither were they simpletons to so misconstrue the New Testament's teaching on Christ if it does *not* teach his deity. Note too that the Roman procurator Pliny the Younger examined the practices of the early Christians and found, among other (harmless) practices, that they sang antiphonal hymns to Christ "as if to a god."[15]

Doing What Is Good (3:1–11)

Remind the people to be subject to rulers (3:1). Paul's instructions regarding submission to rulers and authorities (3:1)—all of whom were undoubtedly pagans at the time—shows that Chris-

---

▶ The Gospel of the Deified Augustus's Birth

There survives a decree of the Roman governor of Asia from 9 B.C. and a corresponding decree of the provincial parliament (the Koinon of Asia) that changed the calendar of the cities of Asia Minor to start on the birthday of the deified Augustus. The texts of these decrees are pieced together primarily from inscriptions found near Priene [a city near Miletus] (OGIS 458). The decree of the Koinon of Asia is particularly interesting because it illustrates the Greek custom of calling the deified emperor a "god" (*theos*), because it uses the term *euangelion* ("good news" or "gospel") for the message of the emperor's birthday, and because it refers to the benefactions of the emperor as "salvation." The Koinon's decree follows in part. (Note that the sometimes awkward translation is due to the characteristic "Asiatic" rhetorical style, which even struck contemporaries as overly grandiloquent.)

Caesar exceeded the hopes of [all] those who received [glad tidings] before us, not only surpassing those who had been [benefactors] before him, but not even [leaving any] hope [of

surpassing him] for those who are to come in the future; and (since) the beginning of glad tidings on his account for the world was the [birthday] of the god, and since Asia decreed in Smyrna, when the proconsul was Lucius Volcacius Tullus [ca. 30–28 B.C.] and the secretary was Pap[ion] from Dios Hieron, that the person who found the greatest honors for the god should have a crown, and Paulus Fabius Maximus the proconsul [ca. 10/9 B.C.], as benefactor of the province having been sent from that (god's) right hand and mind together with the other men through whom he bestowed benefits on the province, the size of which benefits no speech would be adequate to relate, has found something unknown until now to the Greeks for the honor of Augustus, that from Augustus' birthday should begin the time for life—for this reason, with good luck and for (our) salvation, it has been decreed by the Greeks in Asia that the New Year's first month shall begin for all the cities on the ninth day before the Kalends of

continued on next page...

CHRISTIANS ARE TO INFLUENCE for good by doing good and being "peaceable and considerate. . . toward all men" (Titus 3:2). There are no groups whatsoever excluded here: rich, poor; powerful, powerless; men, women, children; black, white—all people are to be approached with equal consideration and respect. And Paul knows the secret of what makes this work: "true humility" (3:2), for it is arrogant pride that leads to inconsiderate and prejudicial behavior toward and slander of others. Paul wishes Titus to model this basic Christian humility for the Cretan church and for us.

tianity is not a social revolutionary religion. Its impact on society should always be profound and good. But it does not engage in revolutionary or bellicose tactics, since Christ's kingdom is not of this world (John 18:36).

God our Savior (3:4). Throughout 3:3–8, Paul uses the title "Savior" twice: once of God (3:4) and once of Christ (3:6); he also reiterates that God has "saved" us (3:5). The words, "Savior," "save," and "salvation" occur proportionally more often in the Pastoral Letters than in other New Testament books, so it was obviously on Paul's mind as he himself faced further imprisonment or was already in custody facing trial.[16] But the focus of most of the

. . . continued

October (September 23), which is the birthday of Augustus.[A-1]

It was a long-standing practice, especially among the Greeks in the East, to ascribe deity or quasi-divine status to mythical heroes, rulers, and others who provided some outstanding benefaction for them (as well as designating them as "savior"; see comments on 1 Tim. 4:10 and Titus 3:4–6). The Romans, on the other hand, were much slower to adopt deification of humans, and only then after they had made a careful linguistic distinction between *deus,* a "god" of the old pantheon, and *divus,* an officially "deified" human. It is a telling distinction of cultures to note the differences between the Greek East (especially Asia Minor) and Rome on this matter of deification of humans. The Greeks had no qualms whatsoever—they deified the emperors with great enthusiasm, ascribing them the title *theos,* "a god."[A-2] The Romans were much more level-headed, perhaps even cynical, about the whole affair. Deification of an emperor or of others was done by an official decree of the Roman Senate in the same way that a person's memory might be

obliterated through *damnatio memoriae* ("Condemnation of one's memory")—an official obliteration of the records of a person's existence.

Still, not all Romans were convinced that the Senate could actually deify someone. The Emperor Vespasian, on his deathbed, is said to have quipped as the end approached: "Oh dear! I must be turning into a god."[A-3] In addition, a bitingly satirical pamphlet thought to have been produced by Seneca right after Claudius's death, turned the "deification" (Gk. *apotheosis*) of Claudius into his "Pumpkinification" (Gk. *apocolocyntosis*)! Such are not the acts of people who take deification seriously.

For Paul the Jew, however, given all the strong emphasis on the oneness of God, which all Jews maintained over against their polytheistic neighbors, it comes as a profound revelation that he ascribes divine identity to Jesus Christ. A fully Trinitarian view is where Paul and the other NT writers clearly lead, as the church's best theologians throughout the centuries have always acknowledged. This is part of what Titus is to "teach . . . encourage and rebuke with all authority" (Titus 2:15).

references to the salvation wrought by our Savior is different from what one normally finds in Greco-Roman antiquity, so we should look into this a little more fully.

Both gods and men were commonly called "saviors" in the Greek and Roman world (cf. comments on 1 Tim. 4:10). But the "salvation" referenced by the title "savior" and the "saving" they did to earn it were usually some benefaction or deliverance from danger in this life rather than a salvation from God's wrath and judgment as found in the Bible (e.g., Rom. 5:9; Heb. 9:27; see Apion's letter given in the box below). The Greek and Roman gods did not all act as judges, and the notion of a final judgment was not universally accepted in Greco-Roman religious conceptions. Many of the gods were known as "savior" gods and were given that title (e.g., Artemis Soteira, or "Savioress"), but Zeus in particular was given the title of "savior," and local varieties of Zeus were often known as Zeus Soter ("savior") or Zeus Soterios ("the Saving One").

Avoid foolish controversies (3:9). As he had similarly warned Timothy (see esp. comments on 1 Tim. 1:4), Paul now

▶ Savior Gods of the Pagan World

The following papyrus letter from the second century A.D. illustrates both the mention of a god who saved from shipwreck and other items found in ancient letters. The letter comes from an Egyptian who has just joined the Roman navy, writing back to his father on safe arrival at the Roman port of Misenum. (His given name is Apion, but the Romans have given him the new name, "Anthony the Great.") The god who was thought to save this fellow was the Egyptian god Serapis (also spelled "Sarapis"), the consort of Isis and often assimilated to another god, Osiris. The letter reads as follows:

Apion to Epimachus, his father and lord, very many greetings. Before all else I pray for your health and that you may always be well and prosperous, together with my sister and her daughter and my brother. I thank the lord Serapis that when I was in danger at sea he straightway saved [Gk. *sōzō*] me. On arriving at Misenum I received from Caesar three gold pieces for traveling expenses. And it is well with me. Now I ask you, my lord and father, write me a letter, telling me first of your welfare [Gk. *sōtēria*], secondly of my brother's and sister's, and enabling me thirdly to make obeisance before your handwriting, because you

educated me well and I hope thereby to have quick advancement, if the gods so will. Give many salutations to Capiton and my brother and sister and Serenilla and my friends. I have sent you by Euctemon a portrait of myself. My name is Antonius Maximus, my company the Athenonica. I pray for your health. (B.G.U. 423; LCL trans.)

Men too were frequently called "saviors" in antiquity. Some men took the title on themselves; for example, a certain Milchos saved Nero's life during an assassination conspiracy and thereafter adopted the title "savior" as part of his name.[A-4] But more often the title "savior" was bestowed as a mark of honor by individuals or communities on someone who had done them some signal service. For instance, in an inscription originating from Metropolis, a village near Ephesus, the community declared Sextus Appuleius, proconsul of Asia in 23/22 B.C., as "their own savior" on an honorary statue (*IvE* 3435). Whether Appuleius had aided them in some time of distress or whether he had simply given them some desired privilege or other consideration to earn this title is unknown. In either case, the title denoted that he acted as a patron or benefactor for the community.

REFLECTIONS

NOTE IN THE PARAGRAPH TITUS 3:3–8 that we have the three Persons of the Trinity cooperating in the work of our salvation: the "kindness and love of God our Savior" is the Father (3:4); the Holy Spirit effects the "washing of rebirth and renewal" in our lives (3:5); and it is accomplished by the work of "Jesus Christ our Savior" (3:6). Christianity is a fully Trinitarian religion, focusing on the salvation worked out by all three members of the Trinity (see also Rom. 8:9–11; Heb. 9:14; 1 Peter 1:2 for similar Trinitarian passages). And this "salvation" is not only deliverance from evil in this life, but a gift to us to become heirs of eternal life (Titus 3:7).

warns Titus to avoid "foolish controversies" because they are "unprofitable and useless" (Titus 3:9). People who turn such nonessential issues into the center of our faith are merely being divisive and should be shunned (3:10–11). Note that "genealogies" and "quarrels about the law" point to issues that are not at the center of Christianity's interests.

Final Remarks (3:12–15)

Zenas the lawyer (3:13). Zenas is otherwise unknown. The job title "lawyer" (Gk. *nomikos*) is somewhat analogous to a lawyer of today. A "lawyer" in the Jewish world was a "scribe" who was an expert in the Mosaic law and functioned as a teacher among the Jews (e.g., Matt. 22:35; Luke 10:25 for the same Greek word used of the scribes). In the Roman world, a "lawyer" would often have been an imperial Roman jurist attached to the staff of the emperor or to the staff of a provincial governor. The most famous Roman jurist is Justinian, whose collections and digest of Roman law in the sixth century A.D. form a major source of our knowledge of earlier Roman jurisprudence. Zenas was probably a Roman jurist in some capacity rather than what we would think of today as a trial lawyer.

Apollos (3:13). Apollos is a colleague of Zenas and is undoubtedly the Alexandrian Jew known from Acts 18–19 and from 1 Corinthians. That he was still active at this later date shows just how sketchy is our knowledge of the exact movements of the apostles and their associates in the earliest church period.

Grace be with you all (3:15). As we find with most letters in antiquity, Paul ends this letter with greetings from others and from himself to Titus and the church in Crete (see the letter of Apion given in a box above). He puts the finishing touches on his greetings with the benediction: "Grace be with you all," showing with the plural reference here that he expects others to profit from the reading of this letter besides Titus himself.

◀

GREECE

Nicopolis was on the western side of Greece in the territory of Epirus.

ANNOTATED BIBLIOGRAPHY

Dibelius, Martin, and Hans Conzelmann. *The Pastoral Epistles*. Hermeneia. Philadelphia: Fortress, 1972.

This critical commentary relies on the typical reasons for rejecting Pauline authorship of the Pastorals, but helpfully gives detailed attention to the historical background and especially connections of the Pastoral Letters with the Hellenistic world.

Fee, Gordon D. *1 and 2 Timothy, Titus*. GNC. San Francisco: Harper & Row, 1984.

This is a concise commentary by a well-regarded NT and text-critical scholar in a popular format.

Guthrie, Donald. *The Pastoral Epistles: An Introduction and Commentary*. TNTC. Leicester and Grand Rapids: InterVarsity and Eerdmans, 1990 (rev. ed.).

A solid though brief commentary by a senior evangelical NT scholar.

Kelly, J. N. D. *A Commentary on the Pastoral Epistles*. TC. London: A. & C. Black, 1963; reprinted Grand Rapids: Baker, 1981.

This brief commentary sticks closely to the text and is marked by Kelly's characteristic sound judgment. Kelly is well versed in original sources and has produced a number of standard works in the later development of early Christianity, which add depth to his commentary.

Kidd, Reggie M. *Wealth and Beneficence in the Pastoral Epistles: A "Bourgeois" Form of Early Christianity?* Atlanta: Scholars, 1990.

This is the best of many such studies on the contemporary social and ethical background of the Pastoral Letters. Kidd surveys an extensive range of background material in this work.

Knight, George W. III. *Commentary on the Pastoral Epistles*. NIGTC. Grand Rapids and Carlisle: Eerdmans and Paternoster, 1992.

This detailed commentary on the Greek text of the Pastorals often gives illuminating historical insights as well as careful attention to the meaning of the grammar and language of the biblical text. The best technical commentary on the Pastorals in print today.

Lau, Andrew L. *Manifest in Flesh: The Epiphany Christology of the Pastoral Epistles*. WUNT 2/86. Tübingen: J. C. B. Mohr (Paul Siebeck), 1996.

This specialized study draws especially helpful connections between the epiphany material in the Pastorals with the OT and other Jewish literature.

Oden, Thomas C. *First and Second Timothy and Titus*. Interpretation. Louisville: John Knox, 1989.

Oden presents an elegant and sane defense of Pauline authorship in this topically arranged "commentary." There are a few rough spots regarding historical background of the biblical world (e.g., sacred prostitution at Ephesus, p. 95), but Oden augments his own helpful insights with a sprinkling of quotations of church fathers and Reformers, which gives the reader a wider view of the interpretation of the Pastoral Letters.

Young, Frances. *The Theology of the Pastoral Letters*. NTT. Cambridge: Cambridge Univ. Press, 1994.

This volume in a promising series spends considerable time trying to establish pseudonymous authorship of the Pastorals. Nevertheless, Young usefully reports on historical backgrounds of the Pastorals in places—for instance, on "teaching and learning in the ancient world" (pp. 79–84), though it seems mostly secondary and derivative.

Main Text Notes

1. See Acts 20:4; Eph. 6:21; Col. 4:7; 2 Tim. 4:12; Titus 3:12.
2. For instance, Clement of Alexandria's *Exhortation to the Greeks*, 1–2.
3. Dio Chrysostom, *Orations* 15.8.
4. Cf. Lacy, *Family*, 108–9.
5. Juvenal, *Satires* 8.
6. Dio Chrysostom, *Orations* 15.5.
7. See Demosthenes' speech *Against Neaira*. For an important recent study related to this issue see Jennifer A. Glancy, "Obstacles to Slaves' Participation in the Corinthian Church," *JBL* 117 (1998): 481–501.
8. Pliny, *Ep.* 3.14.
9. Callimachus, *Hymn to Zeus* 8.
10. The text and translation are from *New Docs* 4 (1987): 151–52; cf. *New Docs* 6 (1992): 18–22 for more on this topic and recent bibliography.
11. The *ius trium liberorum*. See Pliny, *Ep.* 10.2; cf. 2.13; Tacitus, *Ann.* 15.19.
12. Many other examples from Greek and Roman comedy could be adduced. The slave Sceparnio is a good instance from the Roman comic play *The Rope* (*Rudens*) by Plautus (ca. 211 B.C.).
13. E.g., Martin Dibelius and Hans Conzelmann, *The Pastoral Epistles* (Hermeneia; Philadelphia: Fortress, 1972), 143.
14. *Romans* 3.3; *Polycarp* 8.3; cf. *Smyrnaeans* 1.1 (and one ms. at 10.1); *Romans* 6.3; *Magnesians* 6.1; cf. John 1:1.
15. Pliny, *Ep.* 10.96.
16. See W. Foerster, "σῴζω," *TDNT*, 7:965–1024.

Sidebar and Chart Notes

A-1. Translation by Robert K. Sherk, *Rome and the Greek East to the Death of Augustus* (Cambridge: Cambridge Univ. Press, 1984), 125–26.
A-2. See S. R. F. Price, *Rituals and Power: The Roman Imperial Cult in Asia Minor* (Cambridge: Cambridge Univ. Press, 1984).
A-3. Suetonius, *Vespasian* 23.
A-4. Tacitus, *Ann.* 15.71.3.

CREDITS FOR PHOTOS AND MAPS

ALSO AVAILABLE

Matthew

Michael J. Wilkins

Clinton E. Arnold *general editor*

Mark

David E. Garland

Clinton E. Arnold *general editor*

Luke

Mark L. Strauss

Clinton E. Arnold *general editor*

John

Andreas J. Köstenberger

Clinton E. Arnold *general editor*

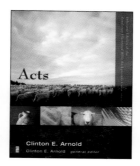

Acts

Clinton E. Arnold

Clinton E. Arnold *general editor*

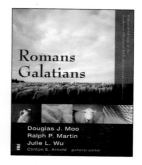

Romans
Galatians

Douglas J. Moo
Ralph P. Martin
Julie L. Wu

Clinton E. Arnold *general editor*

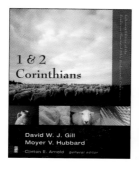

1 & 2
Corinthians

David W. J. Gill
Moyer V. Hubbard

Clinton E. Arnold *general editor*

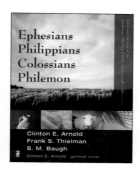

Ephesians
Philippians
Colossians
Philemon

Clinton E. Arnold
Frank S. Thielman
S. M. Baugh

Clinton E. Arnold *general editor*

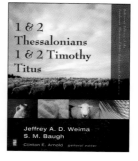

1 & 2
Thessalonians
1 & 2 Timothy
Titus

Jeffrey A. D. Weima
S. M. Baugh

Clinton E. Arnold *general editor*

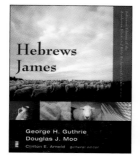

Hebrews
James

George H. Guthrie
Douglas J. Moo

Clinton E. Arnold *general editor*

1 & 2 Peter
1, 2, & 3 John
Jude

Peter H. Davids
Douglas J. Moo
Robert W. Yarbrough

Clinton E. Arnold *general editor*

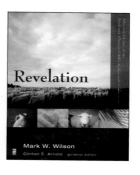

Revelation

Mark W. Wilson

Clinton E. Arnold *general editor*

We want to hear from you. Please send your comments about this book to us in care of zreview@zondervan.com. Thank you.